> I HOPE
> OUR LITTLE
> THESE ARE FROM
> MY PEERS HERE IN F.C.
> SOME ARE EVEN NATIONALLY
> KNOWN (AND BEYOND!)
>
> David

Gathering
WRITERS OF WILLIAMSON COUNTY

Gathering
WRITERS OF WILLIAMSON COUNTY

Edited by Currie Alexander Powers
and Kathy Hardy Rhodes

CPO
PUBLISHING
Franklin, Tennessee

Copyright © 2009 Williamson County Council for the Written Word
Published by CPO Publishing, a Waynick Book Group Co.
101 Forrest Crossing Boulevard, Suite 100, Franklin, Tennessee 37064.
All rights reserved.
No part of this book may be used or reproduced in any
manner without written permission except in the case of brief quotations
embodied in critical articles or reviews.

First Printing 2009
Printed in the United States of America
10 9 8 7 6 5 4 3 2 1
ISBN-13: 978-1-59186-469-1

Library of Congress Cataloging-in-Publication Data

Gathering : writers of Williamson County / edited by Currie Alexander Powers
and Kathy Hardy Rhodes.
p. cm.
ISBN 978-1-59186-469-1
1. American literature--Tennessee--Williamson County. 2. Williamson County (Tenn.)--Literary collections. I. Powers, Currie Alexander. II. Rhodes, Kathy Hardy. III. Title.

PS558.T2G37 2009
810'.8'09768--dc22

2009023333

Book Design: Marc Pewitt
Cover: Powerhouse Inc!!!

The following stories have been previously published:
"The Wild Horses of the Pryor Mountains" by James Crutchfield. © James Crutchfield. Reprinted with permission of the author.
"Wet Stump" by Tom T. Hall. First published in *The Acts of Life* (University of Arkansas Press). © 1985, 1986 Tom T. Hall. Reprinted with permission of the publisher.
"At Ease" and "The River" by Susie Sims Irvin. First published in *Clouds for the Table* (Meetinghouse Books/Providence House). © 2001 Susie Sims Irvin. Reprinted with permission of the author.
"Sim Denny" by Madison Jones. First published in *Season of the Strangler* (Doubleday). © 1982 Madison Jones. Reprinted with permission of the author.
"The Hills of Boston" by Bill Peach. First published in *The South Side of Boston* (Providence House). © 1995 Bill Peach. Reprinted with permission of the author.
"The Willing and the Unwilling" by Bill Peach. First published in *Politics, Preaching & Philosophy* (Published by Westview). © 2009 Bill Peach. Reprinted with permission of the author.
"Pickles" by Paula Wall. First published in *If I Were a Man, I'd Marry Me* (Ballantine). © 1999 Paula Wall. Reprinted with permission of the author.
"June 1864" from the forthcoming novel *Devil's Dream* (Pantheon) by Madison Smartt Bell. © 2009 Madison Smartt Bell. Printed with permission of the author.

CONTENTS

Preface 1
  Currie Alexander Powers

Introduction 5
  Kathy Hardy Rhodes

At Ease 11
  Susie Sims Irvin

The Hills of Boston 13
  Bill Peach

Pickles 17
  Paula Wall

Stick a Fork in Me 21
  Currie Alexander Powers

The Last Pump 25
  Kathy Hardy Rhodes

Wet Stump 27
  Tom T. Hall

Fishing 33
  David B. Stewart

The Young White Cow 41
  Nancy Evelyn Allen

The Toppling of Dominoes 45
  Kathy Hardy Rhodes

Contents

June 1864   49
Madison Smartt Bell

Susan   65
Laurie Michaud-Kay

I Think I Attract the Mentally Ill   73
Robert Hicks

For the Respect of Family and Friends   79
Carroll Chambers Moth

Sim Denny   83
Madison Percy Jones

Secrets of Southern Front Porches   99
Nancy Fletcher-Blume

The Willing and the Unwilling   107
Bill Peach

Raising Eyebrows   111
Laurie Michaud-Kay

Water from Heaven   115
Chance Chambers

Finger Diamonds   121
Nancy Fletcher-Blume

Two Weddings, Four Divorces, and One Marriage   123
Ginger Manley

Tuesday Rendezvous   127
  Angela Britnell

The Trauma, or Real Men Get Facials   131
  Christopher Allen

Losing Richard   137
  Currie Alexander Powers

An Inquiry Regarding Louchelle Maxine Green   143
  Carroll Chambers Moth

Faith   147
  James E. Robinson

Selma, Going On   153
  Christopher Allen

The Cloths of Heaven   157
  Alana White

Face of a Nun   169
  Mary Ann Weakley

The Cowboy Tie   179
  Susie Dunham

The Photograph   183
  Jim Taulman

The Buttermilk Goblet   187
  Linda McClure Dunn

Contents

Medical Miracles *Ginger Manley*	*191*
Sarah's Choice *Angela Britnell*	*195*
Consignment Store *S. R. Lee*	*199*
The Unriddler *Olive Mayger*	*209*
Long Shadows *Louise Colln*	*211*
The Wild Horses of the Pryor Mountains *James A. Crutchfield*	*217*
Minnie Pearl, Price Tags, and Typewriters *Suzanne Brunson*	*219*
The Reluctant Writer *Rick Warwick*	*225*
Find the Good *Alana White*	*227*
One Little Pale-Face Indian Girl *Dorris Callicott Douglass*	*231*
The River *Susie Sims Irvin*	*235*
About the Authors	*237*

PREFACE

As I sat down to write the preface for this book, pondering how this collection of stories came to be, I thought of the adage "It takes a village to raise a child."

Our village is Williamson County, and more specifically, the Williamson County Council for the Written Word. This child, *Gathering: Writers of Williamson County*, is the best of all of us. It has Bill Peach's eyes, Louise Colln's nose, Carroll Moth's chin, Nancy Fletcher-Blume's Southern charm, Sally Lee's eloquence, and the blood of 31 writers running in its veins.

Like many ideas, it began innocently—a rush of excitement, unprimed expectations, the book, in reality outside our normal province as a writing organization. It happened at a Council for the Written Word meeting one February night in 2008. I remember it was bitterly cold and we'd been moved out of our usual meeting room at St. Paul's Episcopal Church because the floors were being waxed. The heat wasn't working in the substitute room—I distinctly remember, as I sat down, hearing the vinyl on the recliner *crackle* like it was frozen. There was just a handful of us that night, those crazy enough to brave the cold, and we sat shivering, anxious to get the meeting started and be done so we could run out to our cars and put the heaters on full blast. An idea had been tossed around about doing an anthology. It was on the agenda, and we were asked for a show of hands to volunteer getting the project off the ground. I'm thinking Kathy and I were losing the feeling in our fingers and may have simply been throwing our arms in the air in an effort to get the circulation going, but there it was, two hands raised in what looked like two people very eager to volunteer to get this anthology started. I do remember a look passing between us. May have been shock, fear, or that strange moment when you realize you've just committed to something you haven't thought through. Then we both shrugged. *How hard could it be?* The council is chock-full of talented writers. Most probably had gems lying around in their desks. We'd pull them together and *presto,* have a book.

We may have been delusional due to the cold.

Or feeling a false sense of bravery because we hadn't actually entered the battle or seen the scope of the theatre.

A year later, we are putting the finishing touches on *Gathering: Writers of Williamson County*. Many meetings at the Franklin Chop House, Barnes & Noble, and Merridees have passed, all the stories have been edited, proofed, re-proofed, bios pulled together, the cover designed, and . . . I pause now to look back in amazement. The seed became a life, and as we read the stories one by one, it grew, took shape, each writer a different color added to the mix, the pages expanding till we had 42 exquisite blooms—a book.

An anthology can be timeless, a documentation of a place and its people. It can also be a fresh piece of literature where the reader discovers a new writer and finds a new friend. Whichever people find, this is a book that represents the incredible wealth of talent, whether proven or untapped, in this corner of the map.

As the stories for *Gathering* were being edited, Nancy Fletcher-Blume and I had lunch with Robert Hicks. Robert had just published a wonderful anthology of stories by Music Row songwriters and I asked his advice on how to compile a collection of diverse stories by so many different writers. His answer was simple. "Just make every writer shine." That is what we have tried to do with this collection—make all the stories shine like the gems they are.

I want to take time here to acknowledge the "village" that raised this book.

We began with an amazing Steering Committee who acted as midwives. Bill Peach, Louise Colln, Nancy Fletcher-Blume, Kathy Rhodes, and I had many planning sessions, assembling committees, assigning duties, and talking about our amazing community of writers.

Next we formed a Selection Committee of the same people, plus the invaluable Angela Britnell, to pick the stories, and spent

PREFACE

many days and nights sitting around the café at Barnes & Noble, or the courtyard at The Factory, poring over the submissions, many of which we loved so much we'd continue discussing them by e-mail for days afterward.

We had an incredible editing team working with the co-editors. They gave selflessly of their time and helped polish these stories till they shone: Louise Colln, Alana White, Jim Taulman—and I want to make special note of Christopher Allen, who passed along his edits via e-mail from Munich, Germany.

Nancy Allen helped round up our Hall of Fame writers, all of whom we are incredibly honored to share the pages with.

The Cover Committee helped put the clothes on these stories. From Olive Mayger, who got the ball rolling, to Mary Ann Weakley, Susie Dunham, and Angela Britnell who helped pick out the shirt, pants, and shoes.

Editor Kathryn Knight deserves high praise for going over the manuscript with a fine-tooth comb. And for helping us name this child.

The book wouldn't have had a home if not for Nancy Fletcher-Blume who spearheaded the march to CPO Publishing so we could consult about our "idea" with her friend Roger Waynick. We went simply for advice and came out of the meeting with a home for our book. Many thanks to Roger and all the wonderful people at CPO Publishing.

Lastly, I want to thank my co-editor, Kathy Hardy Rhodes. We spent many days forced to communicate back and forth in cyberspace, so we'd pretend we were sitting across the desk from one another. This past year has had many ups and downs, personally and professionally, but we soldiered through the rough patches and celebrated when we got an unexpected gift—and there were many. I can't imagine a better partner to work with. Her vision and focus never wavered, and she's a true blue artist, heart and soul.

3

As an endnote, I wanted to mention something I have pondered a lot over the last year working on a book that contains *Writers of Williamson County*. When I moved to Nashville eleven years ago, I sought out the writing community and was immediately drawn to Williamson County. It seemed to be ground zero for all things literary, from the unflagging support shown by Joel and Carol Tomlin at Landmark Booksellers; to the incredible history of writers as evidenced in the bibliography, *Williamson County Celebrates the Written Word*; to the awesome Janice Keck, who as director of the Williamson County Public Library always had her pulse on what was happening in the writing community. There were the writers' nights at Barnes & Noble in Cool Springs where I met many of the writers. Through that, I joined the Council for the Written Word. I never really questioned the fact that I had become a member of the Williamson County writing community. I avoided the obvious. I live in Davidson County. What I have realized, upon reflection, is that the Williamson County writing community is so rich and deep, that despite the fact that I live in Nashville, a city of greater size (and likely a larger writing community), I was drawn to that wonderful place south on 65. So . . . while my house may be in Davidson County, my *home* is in Williamson County. And I am grateful that the writers there have allowed me to be a member of their community.

Currie Alexander Powers
Co-editor, *Gathering: Writers of Williamson County*

INTRODUCTION

Williamson County, Tennessee—just across the line from Nashville. Steeped in history and tradition, it is also vibrant and progressive, known for its scenic beauty, quiet neighborhoods, and thriving business districts. It has been ranked among the top twenty wealthiest counties, as well as the 100 fastest growing, in the country.

In 1799 Franklin, the county seat, was founded, and it stayed a small agricultural community for its first 180 years. The 1980s initiated a period of radical change and growth, as people from all points of the compass began migrating here to live and work. The past twenty years have witnessed a doubling in population. Now a unique blend of history and progress, Franklin is rich with small-town charm and big-city sophistication, from its quaint downtown shopping district to the sprawl of nearby Cool Springs with its Galleria and hosts of other shopping offerings.

In 1988 on the cusp of growth, I came to this Place. I was a child of Delta flatlands and cotton and stale bayous and nothing else. This Place quickly captured me—its narrow backroads that slide through tunnels of saplings and ancient trees, blooming honeysuckle vines, and wildflowers like buttercups and clover and Queen Anne's Lace; centuries-old low stone fences that follow the roadways and lines of sweet yellow daffodils that mark off homesites long gone; Main Street's charm in old establishments like Batey's, Gray's Drugs, the old theater that brought popcorn and Coke to your seat; and local writer Bill Peach standing against a signpost on the corner of Fourth and Main in front of Pigg & Peach, selling suits, selling his books. In this Place, even now, no matter where I venture, I see pastureland on rolling hills and big rolls of hay and old barns and black-and-white cows chewing grass and horses looking over black fences and new subdivisions with lines of old pasture trees and deer grazing in front yards, and the brown, rocky Harpeth River coiling through it all. Yes, this Place is rich.

The year 1988 also brought the founding of the Williamson County Arts Council, along with its literary division, which became the Council for the Written Word.

In October 1999 CWW was established as a separate non-profit organization with a mission of promoting the art of writing in Williamson County—encouraging, educating, and empowering writers. Its first slate of officers included Nancy Fletcher-Blume, President; Mary Lou Bruder, Vice-President; Louise Colln, Secretary; Janet McKeown, Treasurer. Its first Board of Directors included Clay Stafford (Chairman), Nancy Fletcher-Blume, Mary Lou Bruder, Paul Nowak, and Bill Peach, who became Chairman of the Board in 2000. Others drawn in during CWW's first year were Charlene Ring, Mary Nell Snoddy, Cate Howard, Karen Pease, and Sally Lee. CWW's stated mission was "to keep a recorded history of the written word in Williamson County by collecting and publishing names and biographies of writers who live or have lived in the county," and to also "recognize the accomplishments of outstanding writers" through a literary Hall of Fame.

In 2009, its tenth year, CWW's membership has climbed to 52, as people keep migrating to this Place—many of them writers. From New York, Texas, Illinois, Oklahoma, Kentucky, Arkansas, Alaska, Louisiana, Michigan, Missouri, Mississippi, Georgia, South Carolina, Florida, Canada, and England, they have come and melded and merged with homefolks to develop and honor the rich literary heritage of this Place.

CWW's primary project is maintaining a Bibliography of every writer who has lived in Williamson County and published a book. *Williamson County Celebrates the Written Word* now boasts about 400 entries and gives CWW the distinction of being the only organization in the state of Tennessee to keep such records for our county. CWW hosts an open writers' critique group twice a month and conducts writers' workshops and seminars, nationally

INTRODUCTION

publicized and drawing from nationally acclaimed authors and professors of writing, such as Appalachian novelist Sharyn McCrumb and Lee Gutkind, the Godfather of Creative Nonfiction. CWW has also established the Jane Langston Service Award and a literary Hall of Fame, inducting those writers whose contributions and work have enriched our literary heritage and/or brought recognition to Williamson County. Hall of Fame honorees are Virginia Bowman, William O. Steele (deceased), Madison Jones, James Crutchfield, T. Vance Little (deceased), Madison Smartt Bell, Christine Nobel Govan (deceased), Tom T. Hall, Rick Warwick, Bill Peach, Paula Wall, Susie Sims Irvin, Robert Hicks, and William Carter (2009). Selections from many of these noted writers are included in this volume, such as an essay by Robert Hicks specifically written for this anthology about booksignings for his bestselling novel *The Widow of the South*, and a chapter from a forthcoming novel by Madison Smartt Bell.

From 1999 to 2009 CWW has remained self-sustaining with no funding, underwriting, or assistance, except from other local lovers of the written word: the Williamson County Public Library and Columbia State Community College, which have graciously provided a venue for workshops and seminars, and Landmark Booksellers, which has hosted booksignings for council members as well as pre-seminar receptions. CWW achieves its success through a small but talented and committed pool of volunteers and a dedicated Board of Directors: Kathy Hardy Rhodes, President; Dave Stewart, Vice President; Louise Colln, Secretary; Laurie Michaud-Kay, Treasurer; Suzanne Brunson, Corresponding Secretary; Eddie Moth, Historian; Nancy Fletcher-Blume, Chairman of the Board; Bill Peach, Chairman Emeritus.

In celebration of our tenth birthday, CWW presents *Gathering: Writers of Williamson County* as our literary legacy, offering a showcase for the creative works of our members and Hall of Fame honorees—a blend of emerging and established authors.

This volume is a gathering of writers, all 31 of them distilled into this one Place in time—those who are homefolks and those who came here with experiences of elsewhere, those who are published and those previously unpublished. "Above the slumbers" of this once-tranquil, now teeming town, their voices rise and mount the hills and "ride astride the swells of dwindling pastureland." [Susie Sims Irvin]

This volume is a gathering of words and lines that form fiction and creative nonfiction—42 titles rich in qualities readers treasure in Southern literature: a sense of place and character; a love of the land; an appreciation of language, humor, and tradition. These stories evoke themes of change, loss and death, discovery and disappointment, despair and hope.

"Words gathered here form the bouquet of carefully selected arrangements of thoughts and dreams. In our diversity of writers and their works, the Council for the Written Word proudly celebrates and reflects Williamson County," says Nancy Fletcher-Blume, Chairman of the Board.

May Williamson County be proud to proclaim of our gathering: "These too are yet mine."

To our readers—lovers of story, excerpt, and essay—may you feel the spirit of Williamson County writers and may you savor these selections long after you soak in the last line. May our gathering be your blessing!

Kathy Hardy Rhodes
President, Council for the Written Word
Co-editor, *Gathering: Writers of Williamson County*

*A book is like a garden
carried in the pocket.*
Chinese proverb

SUSIE SIMS IRVIN

At Ease

Above the slumbers of the town
Its crown of hills is rising
Emeralds from nocturnal settings
Roused to float upon the mist
Of a morning just now
Making up its mind.

The hills mount then ride astride
The swells of dwindling pastureland
Begin their circling round and back again
An easy canter undulating across the horizon
Propelling the white-headed town below, its
Unsuspecting hub curled comfortably in the lazy
Unwinding coils of the coffee brown Harpeth River.

Susie Sims Irvin

Unaccustomed as it is to change
The town is waking now
To peer bleary-eyed into a thicket of growth
And it is growing more difficult each year
To keep Main Street corralled in the two blocks
That run from the Post Office
Down to where the Confederate Monument
Stands above it all—at ease,
Seemingly unperturbed as the latest invasion
Creeps over the hills through every pass.

The hills *do not know* what to make
Of that mall—its uncertain lineage—
Who pays her dues up front then sprawls
In unladylike fashion across the company counterpane
Mussing it with garish makeup
Casting her eyes a bit too often at the
Town wallet lying open upon the oak washstand.

The hills do know their time is coming but
Tend to look the other way—out toward
Nashville or Murfreesboro or Columbia
And their problems. They speak to each other
Only of the weather.

2

BILL PEACH

The Hills of Boston

Except for a few houses, barns, and rail fences, Boston looks like it must have looked when God finished it on the sixth day, which must have been a Friday, and I guess it would have been January. Miss Gardner, my first and second grade teacher, said some people used to think the world was flat. Nobody who ever lived between two hills in Boston could have believed that.

When God made the world, his big fingers made low places where the creeks run, and the hills squeezed through the spaces between his fingers when he was trying to make it round. He didn't make it exactly round like that new baseball I wanted at Rose's dime store, where my mother works in the town. He made it more like an old ball that you've been hitting with a tobacco stick.

There is one hill that just almost goes straight up, behind the henhouse, across the creek that comes down from the farm where Bernice and Evie Shaw live. It's on the side of our house where the sun comes up every morning. Mammy, my grandmother, says that direction is east. I don't have to know about east or west, because I know which hill to watch every morning.

The hill on the other side, maybe west, where the sun goes out of sight every night about dark, is across the creek that comes down from the farm where Jack Denton lives. That hill is back in the woods, so my sunsets are two cornfields farther away than my sunrises.

I wish I could walk to the top of that hill and watch the sun go down up close. Granddaddy won't let me be out in the woods after dark because I'm just eight. He doesn't spend much time wondering about things like Mammy does. Mammy would go with me, but he won't let her be in the woods after dark either because she's a woman. There are a lot of things you can't do if you're eight or if you're a woman.

Bobby Shaw told me that he went up to the top of the hill to watch it one day, and the sun actually went down behind the hill on the Whitfield farm, and from our house it just looked like it went down behind our hill.

I heard Miss Gardner tell the sixth grade that the sun didn't move, and the earth turned, and we just couldn't see the sun anymore after dark. I wish I hadn't heard her say that, because now it's different when I watch it. What I thought was the sun going down is just me standing in the wrong place.

The hills that I love to climb, and look at, make my sky not as wide, and I don't get to see as much of it as people somewhere else might, except they don't get to see as many hills.

Mammy read in the *Farmer's Almanac* that people knew when the sun would come up and go down a whole year from now, right to the very minute, and wrote it down. The people who wrote the *Farmer's Almanac* never lived between two hills in Boston.

I still don't know why they call this place Boston. Even Mammy doesn't know. She said that was another thing she wondered about. You can't always tell when Mammy is wondering and when she's thinking. She doesn't talk much. Most of the time you have to listen to her with your eyes. She said that you learned things when you were thinking, but when you were wondering you were just thinking about things that maybe you weren't supposed to know.

Most places have simple names that you can understand, like Mobley's Cut, where somebody made a road through a hill that was too steep to go over in anybody's car or wagon. Another place is called Leiper's Fork because of two brothers named Leiper. Mammy just thinks they named Boston after the other Boston that she showed me on a map. It was way up in the corner and had a star beside it. That map didn't even have our Boston on it. She said it would have been about as wide as a pencil point from Nashville if it had been on that map.

She said they were both spelled the same way, except it was pronounced different if you lived up there. Up there it's pronounced like Byeston, and when we say it, it's like Bawston.

We looked at another map that was just Tennessee and some other things around it. I found Boston on that map. It didn't have a star beside it like the other one. Boston was a little white dot with a black circle around it, because we didn't have as many as five hundred people.

I really don't know how many people live in Boston. Sometimes, people who live in Johnson Hollow or Mobley's Cut might tell somebody they live in Boston, because not everybody knows where Johnson Hollow or Mobley's Cut is.

I think there is a sign on the road showing you how to get to Boston, but there is no sign to tell you if you got there, except on the front of the church. If you didn't know where you were, you never would know you were there.

PAULA WALL

Pickles

"Well, you don't have to worry about me," Mom says, shoulders slumped. "When the time comes, I'll get a little room with a hot plate and a percolator, and I'll be just fine."

Sis and I roll eyes at each other.

Ever since Mom went to visit her friend in the nursing home, she's been treating us like we're going to stuff her into a pull-tight Hefty and haul her down to the landfill.

"Mother," Sis says, "you'll outlive us all."

"Primarily because you're going to irritate us to death before our time," I add.

Under normal circumstances, Sis would be peeling my tongue-lashed body off the wall right about now. But today Mom just stares out the window.

"Do you know what people do with their elderly parents in New York City?" Mom asks as the waitress sets another bowl of Polish pickles down in front of her.

"Trade them to the Cubs?" I ask, taking a sip of coffee.

"They drive them into the country and drop them off like dogs," Mom says sadly.

Taking a long drag off her cigarette, Sis gives this some thought. "Don't they have places for unwanted parents?" Sis asks. "You know, like a dog pound for parents?"

"Home run," I mouth, swinging my imaginary bat.

"In the old days," Mom says as she sadly crunches into a pickle, "people respected their elders."

"In the old days," I say, "Arctic tribes left their parents on icebergs and floated them out to sea."

"But I'm sure they were very respectful about it," Sis adds, blowing smoke out of the corner of her mouth.

"Maybe I'll become a nun," Mom sighs.

"A nun," I nod.

Mom is wearing two-inch spiked heels, pedal pushers, and a ruffled top. The only order of nuns she could get into would be the Holy Sisters of the Chiquita Banana.

Snapping open her purse, Mom pulls out a ragged lipstick-smudged Kleenex and dabs her eyes. No doubt it's the same Kleenex she used at my high school graduation.

Chins resting in our palms, Sis and I watch as Mom carefully unfolds a crumpled wad of tinfoil and proceeds to rub it flat on the table.

"Mom," I finally ask, "what are you doing?"

Picking up the dish of pickles, Mom dumps them onto the tinfoil.

"I take it they don't have Polish dills in your grocery," I say.

"I'm embarrassing my daughters," my mother informs the table next to us.

"You're going to get pickle juice all over everything," I insist.

"I wiped this kid's butt," Mom broadcasts across the restaurant as she reaches across the table and stabs the remains of my kosher, "and she's complaining about pickle juice."

"Mother, I will buy you a jar of pickles."

"This is how it starts," she bellows. "First they throw away the pickles! Then they throw away the mother!"

"I should have joined the Peace Corps when I had the chance," I mumble.

Standing up, Mom leans into my face. "Young lady," she growls, eyebrow arched, "you're still not too big for me to bend over my knee."

"I don't know," Sis says, eyeballing my behind. "It's borderline."

"I'll bury you both!" Mom declares as she storms across the restaurant, waving a handful of stolen Equal and dripping a trail of pickle juice.

"Now, that's the woman we know and love," Sis says proudly.

4

CURRIE ALEXANDER POWERS

Stick a Fork in Me

It was hot as hell outside Target. Wendy stood on the sidewalk by the loading zone, scanning the parking lot for Dean's car. She couldn't feel the fork in her arm, but every time she moved, it waved back and forth, pulling at her shoulder. The tines were embedded an inch deep, just below her elbow, in what should have been the flat muscle of her forearm.

The automatic doors whooshed open behind her. Cold air swept out and wrapped around her sweating legs. A shadow moved toward her.

The elderly man stopped beside her and gaped at her arm. "Sweet Jesus. You okay, lady?"

Wendy looked straight ahead. "I'm fine," she said.

She could feel him staring at the side of her face, a gawking freak-show stare.

"I'm *fine*," Wendy said again.

The man put his hands up and backed away. Wendy watched him walk across the parking lot. He turned to look at her every few feet.

It was the dumbest thing. She'd been in the store looking at flatware, holding the fork in her hand. Someone had dropped a bottle of olive oil on the floor and shoved the broken glass under the lip of the shelf. Wendy took a step, and her feet slid out from under her. The fork stayed vertical long enough for Wendy to land on it, the prongs spearing her forearm. She sat there, her jeans soaking up olive oil, and tried to pull the fork out. It wouldn't budge. Her hand was slick with olive oil and kept slipping off the handle as she wiggled it, twisting it back and forth. She sighed and gave up. Calling management would involve explanations. She pulled out her cell phone and called Dean.

"I got a fork stuck in my arm."

"How the hell did you do that?"

"I'm at Target. Can you come and get me?"

"You can't drive yourself?"

"I have a fork stuck in my arm, Dean. People are starting to stare."

"Oh, for Christ's sake . . ." Dean's voice faded and he hung up.

Dean had moved from Phase Two into Phase Three about a month ago. Wendy missed Phase One. It began after the accident.

When Wendy spotted Dean at B. B. King's down on Second Avenue a year ago, it was love at first sight. His initial coolness melted after a few drinks, and when he took her back to the house he rented with two friends from college, despite his liquory clumsiness, the sex was explosive. His guilty face the next morning might have been a hangover or something else, but he asked her out again. Four dates later, he was cooling off. On the fifth date, he drank too much and started an argument in the car, his hands coming off the wheel ten seconds too long to avoid the tree. Wendy torpedoed through the windshield. Her arm stayed behind.

When she opened her eyes in the hospital, Dean was there, weeping uncontrollably. It was the way he looked at her that made the sacrifice tolerable, his eyes eager to please.

Wendy thought about the saying, *I'd sacrifice life and limb for you*. She hadn't meant to go quite that far.

"Just take care of me," she said.

"You got it," Dean said, fluffing her pillow.

That was Phase One.

It lasted until Wendy got the prosthetic arm. It was pretty realistic looking, had a synthetic material that imitated skin, and it fit the wing of her shoulder comfortably. Dean was interested in the arm at first. He just wouldn't watch her take it off at night. If Wendy wanted to have sex, Dean made her leave it on. Then once, in the throes of passion, she hit him with the arm and broke his nose. He lost interest in sex. That's when Phase Two began.

Dean retreated. When she talked to him, he didn't look at her. He fell into a protracted silence. She found him sitting in the kitchen a few times, in the middle of the night, his face in his hands, crying silently. She made an extra effort to show him how little she missed the arm. But the silence grew.

Phase Three began hopefully. Dean came out of isolation, full of energy. He seemed to notice every little thing she did. They started having spirited discussions before going to bed. Wendy would take off her arm, and Dean would start.

"You know I hate watching you do that."

"Should I go in the closet?"

"I just don't need you reminding me of it every two seconds."

"Well, excuse me."

Wendy would get worked up, blood flowing to her wing, pounding and hot. She relished the sensation, how alive she felt with her veins expanding. The wing would start to flap, beating the air.

"Stop doing that!" Dean would yell.

"Come over here and make me," Wendy challenged.

He never did.

The sun was full in the sky now, beating down on the sidewalk in front of Target like a klieg light. Wendy was thirsty. She looked at her watch. She'd been standing there for forty minutes.

She found a sliver of shade under the brow of the store and sat down on a red bench, the metal hot under her legs.

An hour later she was still sitting there. She called Dean's cell phone. It went to his voice mail immediately, meaning he'd turned his phone off.

Wendy went back into the store and walked to the hardware department. She picked up a pair of pliers and stuck them in her pocket.

In the restroom, she sat in a stall and wrestled with the pliers and the fork. The fork came loose and flew under the stall divider into the next cubicle, which, fortunately, no one was using.

She bought a large Coke, took it outside, and sat down on the bench again.

She called his cell six times in a row. It was still off.

She walked to her car, got in, and sat with the A/C going full blast in her face, wondering if there was going to be a Phase Four.

When she parked in front of the house, she knew immediately he was gone. She opened the door and heard the emptiness echo inside.

The closet was empty, and the bedroom was strewn with the evidence of a hasty packing job.

Wendy sat at the kitchen table, fingering the raised line of holes in her arm, rough little vacancies.

"Well, Dean," she said out loud. "I stuck a fork in me. I guess I'm done."

KATHY HARDY RHODES

The Last Pump

"I'll do it," he says, and scrambles out of the car before I can object.

Even though I am three decades out of my father's care, when I go home for a visit, he considers it his place to ride with me to the service station at the corner of Highway 8 and Bishop Road, pump my gasoline, and pay for it. The car is his domain. *The* car, his car, my mother's car, my car. He makes it his business to check everybody's oil level and to make sure their tires are properly inflated and their tags not expired. He's reached eighty, been doing this a long time, isn't likely to change.

He has already checked my oil. It reminds me of when my son lived with my parents while going to college in their town, and how, when the lad's friends would stop by, Dad would lurk at the front window and wait till the boys slipped in the back door. Then he'd sneak out the front and pop their hoods and make sure there was ample oil.

His hands shake as he removes the nozzle from the gas pump and inserts it. The metals rattle against each other as he tries his best to hold it steady with both hands. The shaking has gotten so bad he can barely carry a cup of coffee from the pot to the table, and we all hold our breath as he moves.

His hair is white as the clouds gathering around us, white as the cotton on stalks across Bishop Road, but his eyes still have the blue of his youth, the same blue as the jeans he wears. The pointy-toed cowboy boots he bought at Williams Brothers Store aim toward the pump, and we stand there together watching the numbers roll, adding up the count, as a breeze blows across the flat fields and brushes our faces.

I look down at his trembling hands, marbled with black spots from blood thinner and brown ones they call "liver spots," though I don't know why. His liver is fine. It is just everything else.

As a child I stood in those hands, my feet flat on his palms, and he'd lift me high in the air and I'd balance, like a cheerleader with a beaming smile and pompoms. Those hands held scissors close to my eyes and cut a straight line of bangs, they filled out my offering envelope for Sunday School, they dealt a dollar allowance every Saturday night.

His father's hands shook, too, and he once told me how his grandfather had palsy so bad, he had to suck his coffee out of a cup with a piece of hollowed-out sugarcane, like a straw. Hand tremors cut right down the Hardy line.

The wind rocks the front section of his hair to the right of the part. His hair is always perfect, sprayed in place with Consort For Men, Extra Hold. He fusses over it and tells us to be sure and get it right when the day comes that he is in his casket, dressed for the viewing—"You only have to fix the right side," he says. "It's all that shows."

He holds the pump firmly to the car until gasoline flows over and out and down the side of my Subaru, down the tire well, like a waterfall with the sound of a trickling flow, onto the concrete, already stained with oil and cigarette butts and chewed-up gum.

"Tha's enough, tha's enough," I say and grab the nozzle to shut it off.

"How'd that happen? I better clean it up."

"No, it's okay. *You* go pay. I'll take care of it."

My own hands shake as I put the nozzle back and wipe up the mess, then toss the soiled paper towel into the garbage. The pungent odor of it stings my nose and makes my eyes water. I can smell it on my hands.

TOM T. HALL

Wet Stump

Now this is hard to explain. You take a four pound test monofilament fishing line and thread it through a number four, short shank fishing hook, double the line back three inches parallel, turn the loose end around the long portion of the line an odd number of times (more than three) and then place the loose end of the line through the small opening at the end of the loop and pull the whole of the thing together to form a perfect fishing hook tie.

A man by the name of Wet Stump taught me to do that. He was superstitious about the odd number of times. If you only turned the line four, six, or any even number of times, the fish would get away. I had respect for the man.

We fished out of James Parson's boat dock on Grover Lake. It was a pretty good-sized lake. There were two hundred miles of shoreline and the water got as deep as two hundred feet.

Wet Stump got his name by believing that fish had an attraction to any stump of a tree that was surrounded by water. He hunted out the stumps in the winter when the water was low and would fish them in the spring when the rains came and the Corps of Engineers would let the water level rise above them.

Wet Stump had been raised in South Africa by his missionary parents. We never could talk about politics or religion. He had the darnedest notions about such things. That's why I was not surprised when he told me he wanted to be cremated when he died, and he wanted me to spread his ashes on Grover Lake. He asked me to do that one morning when the sun was shining and the fish were biting. I didn't expect him to die anyway, so I said I would do it. Besides that, I didn't want to hear any long speeches about cremation and the hereafter.

Wet Stump died all right. He was a retired schoolteacher, and he was bringing a big box of books out of the attic of his house and had a heart attack.

I learned about his death at the boat dock. I was washing my boat when one of the guys came along the boardwalk and said, "Old Wet Stump died last night. Heart attack."

The guy who told me that was a cheater. Wet Stump and I had caught him borrowing fish in a bass tournament one time and he didn't like either of us. He stood there looking at me. He knew I didn't like what he was telling me. I started to say something like, "Well, we all gotta go sometime," or, "Well, it's a quick way to go," but I didn't say anything. I sat there on my boat and looked at him. He said, "How old was he?"

I said I didn't know. The guy stood there another minute looking at me, and he said, "Well, we all gotta go sometime." He walked away.

I can't honestly say I had forgotten what I had promised Wet Stump about throwing his ashes in the lake, but I convinced myself I had.

The phone rang three days later and it was Wet Stump's widow on the line. She got right to the point of the thing. She asked me if Tuesday morning at nine would be all right with me. I got right up front trying to get out of it. I said, "Ma'am, I don't know if I can do it or not."

She said, "Well, how about Wednesday?"

I said, "It's not that I'm busy, I just never did anything like that before."

She turned real huffy. "Well, mister, my husband has never done anything like this before either."

I backed off. "Well, how we gonna go about it?"

She said, "Call the Corps of Engineers and ask them if there are any particular regulations."

I said, "You want me to do that?"

She said, "I got these ashes here. Are you in or out?" I could see her standing there with the ashes in an urn or something. I wanted off the phone so I said, "I'll call you back."

The first person I talked to at the Engineers' office was very nice about it, but she put me through to a man who was very blunt. "Look," he said, "you can't throw anything in that lake. Nothing! The only thing I can let you throw in that lake is a fishhook and it better have a line on it."

I couldn't get any further with the story I wanted to tell him. He said, "Now listen, this is me talkin' personal, but I don't think anybody wants to fish in a graveyard." There was another pause, and then he said, "I can give you a Washington address where you can write to if you want to get more information." I told him I would call him back.

I worried about it a lot. I tried to take a nap and not think about it for a while. It became real important. After an hour or so, I called Wet Stump's widow. I said, "Ma'am, they're not gonna let us do it." I told her an exaggerated version of the phone conversation with the engineer. She sat quiet on the phone for a minute. "Well, you be out there Tuesday morning at nine o'clock and we'll do it anyway." She hung up the phone.

Now here's what goes through a man's mind when he has to do something he never expected he would have to do. Don't show up. What do we owe these people? How did we get involved in this? What if we get arrested, what if we get sick? We editorialize.

Tuesday morning was a nice morning. The day was perfect for fishing. When I got down to the ramp that led out to the boat dock, I was a little bit late. There were seven boats gathered around the gas pumps. Widow Wet Stump was dressed in a black outfit that was tight around her throat. I wore my jeans and sneakers and a tee shirt and was surprised to see the other members of the party dressed in suits and ties.

It was the first time I felt sorry for Wet Stump. He would not have imagined a scene like this. It was eerie looking. I nodded as I went by them to my boat. It started easily and I maneuvered it out into the group. The cheater and Wet Stump's widow led the procession down past the "No Wake" sign. We continued on past the sign at idle speed. I followed along at the rear of the procession. I was either being punished for being late, for not being dressed properly, or for having a dirty boat. I don't know which, but I was guilty of all three.

We more or less circled the boats when we got to what we all called Stump Row. It was a line of hardwood stumps that rose about two feet above the water level in normal season. Wet Stump's widow pulled a sheet of yellowed paper from her purse and said, "You won't understand this, it's in African." She began to read what sounded like The Lord's Prayer. You could kind of tell by the cadence of the thing.

When she finished the reading she reached into the bottom of the boat she was in and lifted a clear plastic bag. It looked like a bag of leftovers. She handed the bag across to a guy who handed it to me. I sat there staring at the bag. The widow said, "Proceed, please."

I pulled one of the corners of the bag loose and sort of unzipped it. I stood in my boat and sprinkled the ashes of my friend alongside the water. I felt a sudden sense of elation to be doing such an honorable thing, keeping a promise of such magnitude.

The widow said, "Thank you all for honoring my husband in a way he thought appropriate."

I sat with my head down as the other boats moved away. A minnow came to the surface and nibbled at the ashes of my friend.

The great and noble deeds of man are probably stories. It completely ruins a good fishing day to dispose of the remains of a pal. It does me no good to see a stern widow in a severe black dress. It is of no value to be reminded of mortality on playgrounds. We drink beer on such days and are acutely aware of the insult.

It was not many days later that I traded my boat for a four-wheel-drive vehicle and turned to hunting.

> *Uncle Hugh:*
> *Enjoy the peace and beauty that is too often hidden by the darkness.*
> *(I think you already do.)*

7

D A V I D B. S T E W A R T

Nancy B. Stewart

Fishing

The station wagon, shrouded in new moon velvet of ebony and smoke, hugged its invisible asphalt track through the mountains. He was exhausted and lost to a flood of emotion that thinned his thoughts of peace at the river. His bone-white knuckles appeared more a part of the steering wheel than of man as he willed the car forward through the night. He had spoken little since leaving home. She remained silent, having nothing to offer but her presence, powerless to change his mind once it had been set. But his mind wasn't set. It had retreated.

He turned the vehicle east from the state highway through limestone cut by the WPA and into the closeness of the forest. His mind led its procession of demons and ghosts up through the hills and down mountain fire-roads toward the sanctuary of the river. The patch of family ground there had always provided calm from cares he was unable to leave behind.

He slowed just uphill of the campsite. A bottle rolled out from under the driver's seat as the car found its place and came to a stop. He felt her gaze as his hand fished for and found the bottle. They had arrived.

"There's still a sandwich in back. You need to eat," he heard, as he offered her the bottle. Wincing at the thought, he withdrew the offering, remembering how she, too, had been unable to eat for so long. She deserved better. Shamed and embarrassed, he turned his face from her, opened the driver-side door, and stumbled out onto the campground.

Tannin-infused dampness of decaying leaves and wood met with the scent of wet cedar and a cool breeze blowing up from the river. It smelled of comfort and home. This was a place as safe as a mother's arms, a place where happiness was recorded and available for recall by a sound, a scent, or a sight. He breathed in the memories and was at peace. The smell of rye whiskey rewound time to the present. He wished that he had been stronger, that she could never have seen him so weak—here of all places.

"You should rest." The sound of her voice caressed his ear.

"You're right," he said. "I guess we should've gotten an earlier start."

The car's headlights beamed as far as the riverbank, playing in the leaves of surrounding trees as they peeked from shadows that cradled the campsite. A pair of eyes glowed out of the darkness near the water's edge and extinguished themselves as a raccoon got back to the business of life, fishing along the riverbank.

"I'll be just a minute," he said. Using the available light, he began to check the campsite. His demons found him alone in the dark. They dragged him beneath the shroud of night. A crushing panic constricted his chest after precious breath bubbled away into the darkness. He gripped the bottle as if it alone could pull him back into light and air. Then, as quickly as they had attacked, the demons slithered away and vaporized into the night. He forced a smile toward the headlights, hoping she hadn't seen his terror, and found his way to the rear of the station wagon to unload.

"I'll have the tent up in no time," he said. "I'll get the blankets out, get a fire going. Then we'll rest. It won't be long now." He squinted in search of her sleeping silhouette through the back glass as he raised the rear hatch and pulled out the tent. Alone, he set up camp.

An unseasonable drizzle fell during the night, slowly drowning the untended fire before dawn. Darkness retreated from slivers of sunlight that sliced beneath the edge of the eastern horizon, cut through the worn velvet of night, and scattered over every imperfection of the crystal surface of the river. Imperfect and damp himself, he stood. Dawn burned through his drunken eyes and pounded its way to the base of his skull before he could summon his arms to shield his face. He whipped his head toward the dimness of the forested campsite, reliving the night and how he had come to be there.

A blanket was visible beneath the flap of the tent opening. He decided to let her sleep. Had he slept? He thought he had. Still, he longed for the sleep of the dead, where nothing else mattered. He struggled to shake off the fatigue of his alcohol-induced haze. His head hurt. Looking toward the water, he realized that he had never really been a morning person anywhere but here.

Shiner minnows darted beneath the moving glass, as distant fins of otherwise unseen lunkers broke the mirrored face of the slow-moving water. He remembered her first visit. She had loved how the sunlight sparkled against the quicksilver of curious shiners nibbling at her toes, darting here and there just beneath the touch of a breath. They'd brought smiles to her face.

"It's still beautiful," he said.

She didn't respond.

The canoe lay alongside the station wagon where he had abandoned it during the night. He had decided it could wait till morning. She hadn't argued.

Perhaps she had eaten something before lying down. Hungry, he found the remains of a sandwich, but food couldn't fill the void still nibbling at his spirit. Something stole beats from his heart, sucked air from his every inspiration.

He laid a rucksack in the canoe. With one hand on the bridle, he began to drag the craft down toward the riverbank. The palm of his hand warmed against the pull of the grit-laden hemp. His foot stumbled through charred wood, and his toes stubbed into a stone lining the fire pit. Blackened ribs of a firewood skeleton crumbled into surrounding ash. A whiskey bottle clinked against the stone.

"Damn it," he cursed, knowing he was sure to have awakened her. She never could be far from him. He felt her watching, knowing she could offer no assistance. His eyes misted, blurring his view as he looked back toward the tent.

From beneath silken lashes, the woman of his dreams surveyed the camp. Her hazel eyes grew indistinguishable from dew-studded leaves, capturing drops of the dawn reflected from the stream. Her coffee-colored hair stirred against the stillness of surrounding tree trunks. Out of place, her fair complexion shone in the dim light beneath the forest canopy—dimness that entombed the morning.

Wiping his eyes, he moved toward the bank. With fluid grace, she followed in silence. He put into the water just below camp. A carp startled from the shallows, thrashed over the rocky bottom, and beckoned him into the glare of the dawn's reflection.

"Just look at it. We should have stayed here. I don't know why we bothered living in the city," he said.

An icy spring fed the river from several miles upstream, its heart hidden deep within cold mountain stone. The morning chill of the shallows left him breathless, rigid, airless. Knee-deep in the slow moving current, he grasped the gunwale and stepped into the canoe. It wobbled more than usual as he settled onto the seat, but he and the boat were at home on this stretch of the river. It had always been a special place, a warm place. He caught her reflection in the water as she joined him. She was his heart and soul. She brought him to the surface of life, to air and warmth.

"I must look like hell," he said. He stretched, pulled the shirt over his head and sopped it in the river. The canoe rocked and settled as he retrieved the shirt, wrung it over his head, and wiped his face. The shock of cold water brought him to life again.

He ran his fingers through wet hair and felt himself more present, though his own reflection remained as gray as the morning fog still blanketing portions of the waterway.

The early sun emblazoned the dark underbellies of low, morning clouds, its flame of persimmon and peach flashing beneath them. Tree-lined shadows protected the far bank. Light sparkled like molten stars in the swirling wake of the paddle as it worked alongside the canoe, folding water back onto itself with the soft caress of a lover. Shiners played in the eddies of each stroke, dancing away as if shy, then rushing back at the sudden loss of each new love, their backs brushing silent against the face of the river.

His thoughts were less stable than the canoe. "Has it been fifteen years?" he asked. The minnows continued their dance beside the craft.

"Ten. You carved my name on that cottonwood back at the campground. It was seventeen months, one week, and two days before you asked me to marry you. Are you forgetting? Surely you aren't forgetting. Has it been so terrible that it seems like fifteen years?" Her reflection giggled at his discomfort. The current teased her image as if a breeze had brushed her hair.

He tried not to remember how long she had been ill, then thrust the paddle deep and pulled against the river. Still strong on him, the scent of rye mounted and rode the breeze. His eye caught her reflection, but it was too soon washed away to a blurred memory. He reached inside the rucksack and took a quick pull from the bottle.

Silent and solemn as a hearse, the bow cut downriver. The school of shiners scattered and then refilled the mirror where she had been. Her reflection reappeared as if raised from the stone-littered bottom of the river. He pulled at the water and looked down on her face before splashing playfully in her direction with the paddle.

"Ten years. Two children. Two dogs. One cat," he said.

Silence.

"Isn't it as if the dream has only begun?" he asked as his voice faded to a thought. He looked downriver, following the current. A perch flashed at the water's surface not far from his daydream.

"It's as full a life as anyone could have hoped for. Fuller than some. I can't say it's not full, but I had hoped for more by now. Maybe I've been greedy. Full is such a relative idea. Funny, isn't it?" he heard her ask.

"Funny? When did you become such a philosopher?" He took another drink, wiped a pale wrist beneath his nose, and dipped the paddle at the school of minnows, their pewter fins caressing her watery cheeks.

The shadow of a cloud interrupted his thinking. Startled, he froze for a moment. The canoe continued its quiet slide downriver. Confusion darkened his face. There had been fewer than two seasons of hope, no more than six months. Buried in a dim veil of shadow and melding into the dark backdrop of the forest, he felt the warmth of the sun vanish. All but one small shiner leaped beyond the dark scrim of their riverborne stage. The straggler lingered, as if concerned for his welfare. Another pull from the bottle and it, too, was gone.

The doctor's diagnosis had come as a shock to both of them. Weeks of travel and testing by specialists confirmed their fears. Friends and family members gasped at the news and covered their mouths with open hands—hands that couldn't capture words of grief fleeing on the next breath. "Not now." "Too young." "Surely there are new treatments." There were always new treatments.

She had accepted her lot and had gone about life until medicines and the disease itself exacted their toll in pounds of flesh. Terrified by what the mirror showed her, she withdrew, refusing to be seen or touched by anyone. The hospital gown had swallowed her gaunt figure whole before he could once again run fingers through her hair, touch her cheek, and kiss her lips. Then, she could once again be seen by all who loved her, who wished the family well and hugged the children close.

The children.

Her reflection spoke again. "You look like you've seen a ghost."

His arms moved through automatic motions of piloting the canoe. His thoughts drifted with the current, unseen and steady. Another stroke of the paddle and the canoe slipped farther downstream, gaining momentum as it neared the center of the channel. Only six feet deep at most during the spring, the water remained cooler and heavier here. The gray stone bottom seemed almost too close. The stones, too neatly arranged, lured his mind toward things he longed for the river to wash from him.

Here and there were occasional fits of life, splashing in the shallows along rocky banks. Ducks waddled into the stream, paddled off, and waved their tails as they dove for breakfast. Life, visible and vibrant, continued uninterrupted all around him, beckoned from everywhere—even from among the silent stones. It would be a struggle to return to where he had been. He wondered if he could ever really return. He was changed.

He still hadn't responded to her. She remained silent. Smaller fish swam the warmer spaces, searching for company and nourishment. The bow broke over another school of shiners that scattered and reformed in the gentle slipstream disappearing alongside the canoe. He toyed at the water with the paddle blade as his thoughts led him deeper into the chill flowing beneath the canoe.

The softness of her voice roused him. "You don't need to worry about the children. They're happy staying with Mother and Daddy. They'll be all right." Her whisper sounded encouraging, yet uncertain of whom it was convincing.

The canoe shuddered as the paddle slipped from his hands. He felt the coolness of water on his shoulder, the press of her hand. He steadied himself, reached for a cigarette, and fumbled in the rucksack for a match. A few of the shiners darted from the slipstream and drifted with the paddle.

"So many of our plans are still ahead of you," she said mournfully. Her words lingered on the water. The river flowed gentle and clear as her voice, and the shiners retreated. She was gone.

Some distance upriver, a bass broke the surface. For the span of a heartbeat, it froze at the apogee of its skyward leap, then fell sidelong with the finality of death.

The canoe came to an abrupt stop. Even when empty, its draft was too deep to pass over the sandbar ahead that became a ford farther downstream. With nothing left inside to hold him up, he slumped to the deck. The empty bottle dropped into the bilge and rolled, catching itself on a thwart. Its spirit was now sole master of the boat.

The current nudged the canoe farther into the sand. Immune to the interruptions of life, water flowed gently around the stubborn new obstacle and rippled across the shallow sand. The river moved as it willed—giving, taking, and renewing. More minnows sparkled in the sunlight near the edge of the sandbar. They resumed their lives and followed the current downriver.

He lay there. Going nowhere.

"I'll always love you," he sobbed to no one. And he would. Crumpled and broken, he slept.

NANCY EVELYN ALLEN

The Young White Cow

It had taken Bill eighty-one years to amass the possessions that would be torn apart and dispersed in a day. But it had to be done. His widow would be unable to keep the farm.

One hundred and fifty acres would be sold in smaller tracts. Nine acres held the pre-Civil War buildings and the home that brought back so many memories for Bill's daughter. She sat on the porch with tears dripping off her chin, thinking of crawling through hay tunnels in the mule barn, milking cows, and riding horses into the sedate back pastures.

The log mule barn would be sold separately, dismantled, and hauled away to another state to be used in the building of a new home. Some of the hewn logs were three feet across, twenty-four feet long, and as hard as stone.

It was as if money were no object. The neighbors bid high. Everyone wanted to own the memories. One neighbor even requested a stump be put on the auction block because she remembered sitting on it, watching "Mr. Bill" work when she was a little girl. Everything from antiques to junk was sold— and gone.

Trixie, the spotted pinto pony, had been bought for Bill's grandchildren when they were two and four. She had been their pet for twenty-five years. Bill had cared for the pony as if she had been worth a million dollars. No one wanted to part with her, but the grandchildren were grown and lived in the city so far away. Without asking or telling the others, Bill's widow sold Trixie outright for two hundred dollars to a stranger because she knew the family could not bear to see her sold at auction. The pony looked back and nickered as if to say good-bye when the buyer loaded her on the truck.

Unaware of their fate, all the cows but one came into the lot for salt. The young white heifer stood beyond the gate, suspicious of the mounting activity near the barn, as if awaiting a familiar voice: the tender "Succor, succor!" call from Bill. The men who were taking care of the sale tried to no avail to coax her into the barn lot with the other cows; yet she stood outside the fence, a still, knowing glare from her big brown eyes penetrating the deceptively peaceful setting.

"You boys get that cow on in here!" shouted the man in charge. Two of the younger helpers went out the side gate, positioning themselves between the cow and the creek. She turned her head, switched her tail, lifted her right foot and turned it out. One of the boys waved a stick and yelled to encourage the pale heifer through the gate. He hardly knew what happened as she streaked past him, tail over her back, running for her life. All they could do was stand and watch as the sagacious white cow was swallowed by the hills, giving way to absence—gone.

Each cow, bull, and calf took its turn in the auction corral.

"Who will start the bidding at three hundred dollars—now four, now five?" cried the auctioneer. One cow and calf even sold for a thousand dollars.

At the end when it looked as if all was said and done, the auctioneer said, "There's one more cow, but she's on the hill. Who will buy the cow on the hill?"

There was no description and no explanation as to why the cow was not present. All was silent and then the final bid.

"Three hundred dollars," a voice came from the back.

"Three hundred it is—sold!" said the auctioneer.

The new owner of the fabled cow was the local veterinarian. He had seen her before and was prepared for a fight. Even as a calf she had been hard to manage.

First, he and the men he brought with him had to find her. They walked up the hill, around the knoll, and over the ridge. There she was, a solitary white speck grazing in a sea of green meadow. They crouched low as if hunting for a wild animal. The heifer barely felt the dart as it entered her side. Tranquil dreams of cool, succulent grass and flowing streams filled her sleeping body as she was safely lifted onto the wagon.

The young white cow now roams the hills of another farmer, where she waits for another encouraging voice to call her to enticing marble mounds of salt, and where there is not yet a need for a corral or a final sale.

KATHY HARDY RHODES

The Toppling of Dominoes

"It'll be a biological desert," the voice on the other end of the phone said, then paused and waited for my reaction.

I looked out the bay window at the blazing yellow and orange maple in my backyard, crispy brown leaves piled up around its stem. I pictured the old family farm the forester was describing, four hundred miles away. It would be a wasteland of bald hills. No vegetation. No wildlife. Acid bubbled up to my throat and burned, and I swallowed hard.

"It'll look like a bomb dropped on it," the forester continued.

I produced the image of torched ruins silhouetted against my bald hills. Remains of scalded tree skeletons and stumps, burned limb parts, all charred and black. White ash powdered over the debris, white smoke rising from it all.

"I'm not going to kid you. It will be ugly. You've probably seen—"

"Yeah, I've seen it before," I said. Driving on Highway 16 toward my fifth-generation family land, I'd seen it off to my left, then to my right up the road—what looked like a nuclear aftermath. Seemed like every landowner was clear-cutting. It sickened me and I told myself I'd never do that. I'd never shave my land, then burn it.

"You've got a lot of trees that are rough—crooked, hollowed, beehived. Those will all go to pulpwood."

Paper. Books. Softcover romances and *Country Living* magazines. The newspaper industry would continue to flourish. People would be reading my trees with their morning coffee. Trees I played in as a child. Hardwoods that shaded the stream where I waded. Pines that blanketed my paths with soft, sienna needles.

"Now, you don't have to do *anything*," he continued. "But if you want to make your land an investment, then sell the timber, clear-cut, burn or spray a herbicide, and reforest as a monoculture pine plantation."

The word "plantation" intrigued me. It sounded so Old South.

"A well-managed pine plantation could bring in three thousand an acre with a timber-cutting," he said.

I calculated how much money that would be for my children in thirty years. Then I factored in the far extreme of what I have now: acres of loblolly pine, oak, elm, maple, sweet gum. Woods "thick as hairs on a dog's back," my father always said. Brush and brambles and tangles of vines covering the forest floor, so thick you can't take a step without getting caught up in them.

I asked a few more questions. I didn't want to let him go. Once I hung up the phone, I'd be a step closer to having to make a decision.

What will happen to the wildlife—abundant deer, rabbits, wild turkeys, squirrels? I once went possum hunting and shot a gun for the first time in those woods.

What will a burn or chemical spray do to the natural spring and the stream that trickles from it and courses through the thickets?

What about the old Choctaw Indian burial ground where seventy-five early natives are buried? Should I disturb the dead?

What about the wild muscadine vines? My ancestors brought cuttings from North Carolina when they migrated in the early 1800s. Growing up, I ate the grapes warm from the vines. I can't bear to lose them.

How could I end it all? One strike of a match, one trigger pull on a chemical spray, and five generations are gone. Dust to dust. Green to ash.

"Think about it," he said, "and let me know."

"I'll think about it." I punched the gray button that beeped, then echoed in my head. He was gone.

Everybody is gone. Everything is slipping away. It is like slow-moving dominoes, one falling away after another, crashing down in a long line until all are gone.

The family structure has disappeared, passed on, and now I must stand on the legacy and either hold it all up or tear it all down.

The land, in family hands since 1850, used to be a working farm. I have the original land deed—words handwritten, now fading, on a piece of paper, now sepia and powdery, worn thin as tissue, so delicate it is coming apart in the folds.

My father grew up on this land. And my grandfather. And great-grandfather. My great-great-grandfather moved here and settled after the stars fell on Alabama.

My father ran barefooted across the pine-needled paths, dug up arrowheads, played in the gullies and gulches. My grandfather plowed fields, planted cotton. My great-grandfather tended apple orchards and sold buckets of sorghum. My great-great-grandfather planted seeds in the red clay soil.

I've walked the same trails as those who went before me.

My grandfather made improvements to the farm back in 1935, when the Soil Conservation Service of the Department of Agriculture taught him how to prevent erosion. Before that, Grandpa was plowing up and down the hills, and dirt was washing away with every big rain. The government taught him contour plowing, making furrows that followed the curves of the land. They showed him how to terrace, cropping on different levels, and plant pasture grasses with dense roots, like lespedeza, white clover, and dallis grass, to stop the precious soil from flowing away. They gave him invasive, drought-resistant trees, like vitex, soapberry, and tree of heaven, designed to prevent erosion. They also gave him two thousand black locust trees to use for fencing his pasture. Grandpa changed the face of the land for the better.

My father cut some timber once, back in 1985, and put five thousand dollars in each grandchild's savings account. The kids all started college on that money. Then he replanted pines with his own hands.

He passed the land on to me, then he passed on. Now I must decide what to do with his land, *my* land.

A biological desert? My cheeks grew hot and stung.

I know the four men who went before me are waiting, watching to see what I will do. Beaman, Thomas, Tyre, Wallace. I picture them standing shoulder to shoulder at the treeline, like sentries, on soil that was worked by their hands for a century and a half, their whispers blowing through the pines behind them, stirring up a big wind.

A tear rolls cold down my face. Then another.

The dominoes have toppled. I'm the only one standing. It's my turn.

When I push the buttons to call the forest resource management company, my words will set a course for the old family land. They will show what kind of steward I am of things ancient and precious and worth more than their value.

MADISON SMARTT BELL

June 1864

Within a glade outside the town they buried two deserters in the rain. A third, a boy in his teens, had at the last moment been spared. Forrest, turning his head to one side to spit into the hoof-churned mud, rasped, *let the young'n live*, and looked as if he might say more, but didn't.

Afterward the boy helped them dig one grave for two. Henri didn't know if he were friend or kin to the two grown men who'd just been shot or if the three of them had ended up in the bottom of the same sack through simple mischance alone. The boy's face was wet as he worked, but maybe only from the rain. Sticky mud clung to shovel blades and would not be shaken loose. When the grave had at last been filled, Benjamin led the boy away toward the shelter of the wagons. Ben's face looked lined and weary from the digging. He said nothing, but guided the boy with a large hand set between his shoulder blades.

That night Henri lay wakeful under the forked canvas of the shebang, knowing from Matthew's stiffness beside him that Matthew wasn't sleeping either. Moisture beaded on the underside of the sodden cloth, soon enough began to drip. Henri pushed his mind away from the two dead men and the young survivor. He would not learn their names or know their faces. Forrest had been in a savage mood for quite some time. The lousy weather might account for some of it. Braxton Bragg, still nominally his commander in spite of all, kept him annoyed with criticism of his recruiting methods, which were indeed sometimes a bit severe, as the dismal events of that day had proved. Since Fort Pillow, the Yankee papers had been painting him with ill repute. They made him out a *mean vindictive cruel and unscrupulous* man who often whipped his slaves to death and kept a black concubine in his house to quarrel with his wife. There were rumors, too, that Negro troops at Memphis had sworn blood vengeance against Forrest and all his men. Worst of all, Forrest's plan to attack Sherman's rear as Sherman moved from Nashville south toward Georgia had been thwarted by as many as ten thousand Federal troops who had come out from Memphis, under command of General Samuel Sturgis, to divert him. For the last eight days they had been playing hide and seek with Sturgis in the rain.

Above the pelting on his peaked square of canvas, Henri heard voices calling across the camp, and presently Bill Witherspoon raised a wet corner of his shebang.

"Come on, boys, let's have some fun!"

The rain was too heavy for Henri to make out Witherspoon's lopsided grin. "What kind of fun?" he said.

"Pea-picking, corn-husking. Find out when we get there. We're all going over to Stubbs Farm."

Beside Henri, Matthew sat up, silent, alert, ready. He checked his pistols in the dark.

"It's wet out there," Henri said.

"No more than it is in here," Witherspoon said. "Come on."

Henri crawled out from under the dripping shebang and shook himself like a wet dog. He exchanged a glance with Matthew in the dark. They went to find their horses. In ten minutes they were riding south from Ripley, Mississippi, treetops sagging under the rain in the groves that fell away down the slopes from the ridge where the road ran. Witherspoon took up a song, his pale face raised into the rain.

JUNE 1864

Come on, boys, let's go find'm
Come on, boys, let's go find'm
Come on, boys, let's go find'm
Way down yonder in the paw-paw patch.

Finally someone shut him up. Then the rain began to slack. On the western horizon was a glimmer of the quarter moon, and through gaps in the clouds came starlight enough to illuminate their exchanges of fire with the Federals camped around Stubbs Farm. More fun than a pea-shelling, Witherspoon considered, except you couldn't meet the girls. At daylight when they rejoined Forrest up at Boonetown, the weather had cleared completely and promised to be very hot, and they were able to say of a near certainty that the enemy was headed down the railroad line through Guntown toward Tupelo, Okolona and the fields of ripening corn on the black prairie there.

"Let's go get'm," Forrest said briefly. He looked haggard in the thin dawn light, his narrow lips buried in tendrils of his untrimmed beard. "Catch'm quick and hit'm hard."

"General," Colonel Rucker said, "he's got eight thousand men over there already, and we've scarce got two."

"When did that kind of a thing start to worry ye?" Forrest snapped. Then in a more considered tone. "It ain't about how many they is. Never was—won't never be. I'd take one of ourn over ten of theirs any day you care to name. Damyankees ain't got thar yet today and they got yet a ways to go. It's comen up hotter'n hell already and oncet they run five miles through that sucken mud they'll be so beat we'll ride right over 'm."

Where's there, Henri thought, exchanging a glance with Witherspoon, and then he thought that maybe he knew. Forrest's orders were to fall away south and join Stephen Lee, perhaps Chalmers also, to defend Okolona and the fields of unharvested grain. But considering last night's reconnaissance they'd have a good chance to find the enemy at a much nearer point, somewhere between Stubbs Farm and Guntown. Last night he, Matthew, Witherspoon, and the rest had returned toward Boonetown across a bridge over Tishomingo Creek, and passed through Brice's Crossroads. There were thickets of blackjack oak all about to cover their approach.

A younger voice piped up. "General Forrest, sir?"

With a shade of impatience Forrest turned his head.

"They say hit's a passel of niggers come out with the Yankees, gon carry you back to Memphis in chains like what you put on them. Say they gon burn you, and skin you alive."

"Boy, that don't make no sense," Forrest replied. "They'd need to skin me afore they burnt me, else they'd not git much of a skin."

No one laughed. Henri, reluctantly, turned his head toward the questioner: the same stripling who'd just escaped the firing squad the day before. His pinched dirty frightened face, like a rat with the plague among them.

"And then they'd need to catch me before they could carry out any part of that plan," Forrest said.

"They say they gon kill everbody." The lad's voice began to shake. "Say they gon kill us all and take no prisoners."

"They can say what they want to," Forrest said, and made to turn his back.

"But do they mean it?"

Forrest rounded on him then. "How the hell should I know if a body means what he says or not? If I was to say it I'd damn sure mean it. That's all I know. The rest we'll find out when we git thar. And I mean to git thar quick."

"All right," the boy said, stepping back; he seemed surprisingly satisfied with the answer. "All right."

They rode south from Booneville on a track west of the rail bed. Beyond the thickets further west, Henri could hear the faint trickling of a stream. It was already very hot, as Forrest had predicted. Now and then a woodpecker tapped at a hollow tree. The staccato drumbeat carried a long way through still air.

"What about us?" Matthew said.

Henri looked over his shoulder.

"I mean what do you think they'd do to us."

"They?"

"The black troops with the Yankees. That wear those badges —*Remember Fort Pillow*."

Henri slowed his horse so that he and Matthew fell a few lengths behind Witherspoon and the other white men of their company. "I doubt many of this bunch were ever at Fort Pillow," he said. "They couldn't have been. You know that." He paused for a moment, recalling the river at sunset, running with blood; at the edges of the great blood slick, threads of blood unraveled in the water, tendrils trying to reach or root in something.

"What is it that they say they remember?" Henri asked. "What really happened or what somebody told them did?"

For a moment Matthew said nothing. He glanced back once at Benjamin, who had left the wagons to Jerry and the other teamsters and was riding in the rear with the arms of a cavalryman in his belt, and on his saddlebow. What really had happened at Fort Pillow, Henri was wondering now. Was there still any autonomous fact of that action, or only the story he'd told himself?

"I don't want to fight my own people," Matthew said.

"Matthew," Henri said. "*Mathieu*. You've come to the wrong war."

In the rear, Ben clucked his tongue.

"You talk like you know who your own people are," Henri said. It struck him that maybe he was being more quarrelsome than comforting, as the crackle of rifle fire began to rip through the blackjack thicket ahead of them. Some of the Federals appeared to be armed with the new Spencer repeating carbines, but these were wont to jam in the heat of a fight, while the navy sixes seldom misfired. Forrest turned out to be correct that the brushy terrain did everything to conceal how few the Rebels were, at this point, in comparison to the enemy.

Henri could not make out the crossroads or the bridge through the thickets. Indeed there was more than one pair of roads that crossed in these few acres east of Tishomingo Creek. As best he could recall from riding a similar route in darkness the night before, the bridge would be maybe half a mile distant. He circled north, with Matthew and Ben, in the direction of the Baldwin Road. They had got separated from Witherspoon, last seen clubbing a Federal trooper with a jammed repeater he'd snatched from another of the enemy.

The booming of two Federal batteries fell away behind them to the south. They were angling, Henri thought, toward the Federal left flank, though it was almost impossible to locate the lines in this heavily wooded ground. Of three hundred fifty men of the Seventh Tennessee, only seventy-five were still on their feet by this time. They fought dismounted now, struggling with Federals firing from cover of a brush fence at the south side of a trampled pasture. More and more Union flags appeared in the woods behind as the Federals brought reinforcements across Tishomingo Creek. Somehow the fighting had already gone on for most of the morning and the Rebels looked as if they were starting to tire.

Then Forrest came cantering up on a dapple gray horse he favored. He'd shed his coat and rolled his sleeves. The double-edged saber flashed in his left hand.

"Git round the left," he shouted at the remnants of the Seventh. "Take the damjobbernowlyankees in the rear there. Git on with ye—if ye're feart to be shot ye best go forward for I'm well and goddam ready to shoot ye in the back if ye don't."

Henri stared as the dapple gray reared up in the middle of the open field, under a hard rain of shrapnel and minié balls. There seemed no possibility that both horse and rider would not instantly be killed. But no. Forrest leaned forward, the horse's front hooves regained the ground, and with a forward sweep of his blade he cried, "I'll lead ye!" The yell went up, behind, then beside him as what was left of the Seventh rushed past Forrest toward the Federals at the fence. Forrest had turned his horse out of the line to ride back to Bell's brigade, which appeared to be retreating before the Yankee reinforcements constantly arriving on the field.

"Come on I tell ye," Forrest screamed. "I tell ye them sonsabitches is too tired to fight. They were whupped before they got here. Git over there and finish'm off." He swatted a man across the shoulders with the flat of his blade. Again the hair-raising yell tore across the field as Bell's brigade charged to join the Seventh. Rebels were jumping the fence now, fighting the Yankees hand to hand. Henri glimpsed Witherspoon again for a moment, gleefully trumping a Federal saber with his pistol. Further back in the woods, the Yankee line reformed for a few minutes, attempting a rally, then as ammunition ran low, it shattered in confusion.

Henri's ears rang in the weird, muffled silence that followed. Presently he began to hear woodpeckers resuming their work, but as if the sound was wrapped in cotton batting. Matthew was walking on rubbery legs back toward him from the battle line, his face streaked with blood and burnt powder, apparently unhurt. Henri discovered he was holding Matthew's horse.

Forrest was riding toward them now, his sword hand low. His coat was draped across the saddle-bow, and his once-white shirt was transparent with sweat. Distant firing broke out behind, a long way off, down in some hollow through the woods toward the creek.

"That'll be Barteau," Forrest grinned. Colonel C.R. Barteau, detached from Bell's brigade, had gone the long way 'round the Federal left to intercept their line of march from Stubbs Farm.

"Where's John Morton?" Forrest raised his sword point toward Henri. Matthew had just now remounted. Henri turned his horse aside. He remembered seeing Morton, who'd dragged his handful of cannons eighteen miles that morning, the last third of that distance at close to a run, coming to support Bell's charge at the end of the most recent action.

"That way," he said, and he and Matthew fell in behind the dapple gray as Forrest rode in the direction indicated. Shortly they came upon the eight small cannons known to everyone now as Morton's Bull Pups. The battery was still taking fire from the Yankees. John Morton's pleasant moon face popped up from behind a gun carriage.

"General Forrest," Morton said. "You had better go further down the hill, for you are apt to be hit where you are now."

Henri had never seen Forrest meet any such advice as that with anything other than furious dismissal. Now he looked irritably about himself, swiping one of his hands through the air as if he could bat down bullets like flies. Then, dropping his hand to his knee, he nodded.

"All right, John. I may rest a while." He rode down the slope where Morton had pointed, and dismounted beneath an old hickory tree. Matthew caught up the loose reins of the dapple gray horse. Forrest took his coat from the saddle-bow, scraped nut hulls aside with the edge of his boot, and spread out his coat between the roots of the tree. He lay down, closed his eyes, and appeared to stop breathing.

Henri, Morton, and Matthew exchanged a weird glance. Maybe, Henri thought, some missile had pierced Forrest's heart without making any visible wound; maybe he would never rise again. They waited for a sign of his breath and saw none. Morton made to speak and didn't. With a forefinger he pressed his lower lip against his bottom teeth.

Inside of two minutes, Forrest sprang up as if he'd been lying on tongues of blue flame.

"Time's a-wasten," he yelled. "This battle's nigh whupped but we still got to whup it. Got to keep after'm, keep up the skeer! Why ain't that whole line chargen already?"

He yanked Morton to him by the upper part of his sleeve. "John," he said. He was holding Morton almost as close as a lover, while with the other hand he gestured. "I want ye to run yore pups straight down that road, and keep'm barken right in their faces, hear me? Give'm hell, John."

"Sir," Morton said, "the guns are subject to be captured if I rush forward that way without support."

"Artillery was made to be captured," Forrest snapped. He gave Morton's upper arm a squeeze and added, with his ragged grin, "I'd like to see anybody capture yours."

The day was waning. As the sun dropped away to the west, long rays of blood-colored light came slantwise through the darkening boles of the trees. They were driving a wedge between the Pontotoc and Baldwyn roads. To his left, Henri could hear the Bull Pups cough and roar, spitting grapeshot at the Yankees at point-blank range.

Somehow another two hours passed. Where the two lanes met at Brice's Crossroads, the Yankees made another stand. Forrest's men charged them till they broke and scattered back to Tishomingo Creek. Henri and Matthew were both carried along in the rush to pursue. Some distance ahead of them a cry went up.

"Here's the damn niggers!"

The black companies they'd all been hearing about had been kept back to guard a cluster of supply wagons drawn up just west of the creek bank. They formed up now in good close order to meet the Rebel rush. The white patches standing out sharp against the blue tunics must be the *Remember Fort Pillow* badges. Excellent target, Henri thought, but his pistols stayed holstered in his belt.

What about us? Matthew had said. The black companies were covering the retreat of the white Federals fleeing from the crossroads of the creek, and doing a determined job of it, too. Though the skirl of the Rebel yell filled Henri's ears, the momentum of the charge had been blunted. Matthew, inexplicably, got down from his horse and began walking into the melee, stiff-legged and empty-handed. Henri got down himself, handed the reins of his horse to Benjamin who had just come up behind, and followed. He was so frightened he wanted to puke. Though their uniforms were so tattered as to be unrecognizable, there could be little doubt about whom they'd rode in with. Yet Matthew seemed to walk robed in his father's untouchability.

Henri followed him through a gap in the line, taking a long step over a corpse still twitching. It was the boy that had asked the question that morning, he thought, who'd been spared the firing squad at the last moment the day before. But he couldn't pause now to look twice and make sure. From a wagon bed someone was sighting one of the new Spencer repeaters on Matthew. Henri's own revolver was cold in his hand. He knew the idea was to take out the rifleman *before* he shot Matthew, but he felt he could not bring himself to do it until afterward. There was something about this enemy's face. Though he did not wear a Fort Pillow badge, he had actually been at Fort Pillow. There he had told Henri his name. Sam Green.

He must have cried the name out loud, for Green lowered his weapon and beckoned the two of them up into the wagon with him. Matthew, still moving stiffly, like an automaton, climbed up behind the right front wheel. Sam Green stretched out a hand to help him. Henri stuck his gun back into his belt and clambered up after. The wagon was loaded with sides of bacon and dried beans in burlap sacks. Somewhere there was a faint odor of coffee. Ginral Jerry would be overjoyed with such a find.

"How've you been," Henri said. The three of them were stretched out now across the bean sacks, keeping their heads below the wagon rails, for there were more than a few bullets singing over them.

"Been all right." Sam Green smoothed a palm over the breech of his Spencer. His palms were gray with calluses that looked like limestone furrowed by water. "Just tryen to live."

Henri found himself trying to think about all the most extreme efforts he had made to live himself, all at the same time. He looked around for something to stop his thoughts. Matthew had turned from the other two men, his body molded over slabs of bacon. He was watching the fight through a crack between two warping boards.

"What about y'all?" Sam Green said.

What about us, Henri thought. It occurred to him that in the end one might betray everything. So that in the end there was no other constant than betrayal. He raised his head to look out of the wagon and very quickly brought it back down.

"They're fighting like there's no tomorrow."

"Cause for us they ain't. Kill or be killed. No mercy nowhere. That's what they believes."

Us or them, Henri thought, then asked him, "Do these Yankees treat you right?"

"Don't know bout that." Sam Green flattened further on his back. His eyes, tobacco-brown in the whites, looked up at the swiftly darkening sky. "They says we ain't slaves no mo but they don't treat us like we men. Don't leave us drink outen they dipper. Don't leave us drink outen they wells. We come across the country taken what we finds anyways we can take it."

"And then they give you a bad name for it."

"Tha's about what they do." Sam Green chuckled softly. In the fairly near distance, a wounded horse screamed. Green turned sideways to squint through the wagon rails. "Colonel Bouton, now, he ain't so much that way. He act like he count on us, most times. Go on and look at him over there now."

Henri raised his head again. There indeed was Edward Bouton commanding with a sure authority, grim but graceful under a flood of fire. Black troops moved willingly to his order, opening their line to let the fleeing Federals through, then closing again to resist pursuit. They disputed every yard of their retreat.

A man with a Fort Pillow badge rushed up to the wagon looking for cartridges and screamed his frustration when he found only beans. With a butcher's knife drawn he ran back to the fight. Horse holders were struggling to hold mules panicking from the racket of battle. Bouton and his black soldiers were fighting ferociously on the right of their line.

"It's hangen for him if y'all catches him, see?" Sam Green remarked. "Ain't no tomorrow for him neither." His head turned suddenly, as if to some specific sound Henri couldn't pick out from the general barrage. Then he jumped out of the front of the wagon and unstaked the two mules hitched to the tongue. Something on Bouton's left had broken and a whole white Federal infantry unit was coming back at a panicked run. Sam Green clucked to his mules, tapped them with a length of cane. The wagon turned, jostling with others as they moved toward the bridge, some drivers lashing each other's mules as they tried to advance. Sam Green, horribly exposed on the wagon box, murmured to his animals more calmly.

It was almost too dark to see anything now. Red flashed from the muzzles of the guns. Some black soldiers now had joined the flight, sailing past like bats in the gloaming, some ripping off Fort Pillow badges as they ran. Others fought on desperately. Sam Green patiently maneuvered the wagon onto the first boards of the bridge. Then the tiny movement he'd been so carefully conserving altogether stopped. Ahead of them the bridge was blocked by a wagon jammed crossways.

Sam Green craned his neck to peer ahead of him, then behind. Henri followed the direction of his backward glance. In the

JUNE 1864

darkness by the tree line a muzzle flashed red and he saw the ball lift from the barrel and arc toward them like a meteorite, growing till it blotted out the sky. A kind of astral music accompanied it, ringing, shimmering: the music of the spheres. The bullet moved with a terrible dark lethargy toward them, but Henri could not seem to move any faster. He wanted to snatch Green out of the way, while his arms felt like they were trapped in molasses. He was himself bound to the pace of this world that embraced him in its awful slowness. The bullet lumbered into Sam Green's left temple before Henri could reach him, and he pulled him down among the sacks already dead.

Matthew rolled over and opened Green's collar, feeling around his throat for a pulse. Henri watched blood soaking through the burlap under the dead man's head, trickling down among hard pellets of white beans. Events resumed their previous hectic speed. Some of the routed Federals were pausing to set supply wagons on fire before flinging themselves into Tishomingo Creek. Some of Forrest's units had crossed ahead of them, upstream, and were picking the Yankees off as they tried to come out of the water on the other side.

Then Forrest himself rode clattering onto the bridge, eyes flashing yellow like a wildcat's. "Bytheblackflamenassholeofthe-Devilhisselftheseshitsuckendamyankees're burnen my wagons, goddammit!" he shouted.

Oh, Henri thought, they're your wagons now.

"Git up, son," Forrest said to Matthew. "You can't jist lay thar. That man is dead."

Matthew took his hand from Sam Green's throat and straightened as if waking from a dream. "Where's Willie?" he said.

"I don't know," Henri said. "I haven't seen him. I don't think he's here."

Forrest had already passed them, was directing a squad of men to heave the jammed wagon out of its place and tumble it

61

over into the stream. More men of their company flowed over Sam Green's wagon, carrying away the bacon and beans, automatic as a file of ants. Sam Green's body flopped onto a few wisps of straw that still lay on the stripped boards of the wagon bed. Then Benjamin's grave face appeared above the rails. Matthew got out and took the reins of the two horses Benjamin had led back to them. Benjamin pulled Sam Green's ankles to straighten his body, then folded the dead man's hands across his breastbone. Other men were already lifting the wagon clear of the bridge, releasing it above the creek. It fell straight down, the wheels grooving into the surface of the water. Henri was somehow back in his saddle without quite knowing how he had got there. He leaned to see water filling the wagon bed, so that Green's body floated calm and free for a moment, still within the frame of the rails. Then the wagon spiraled away in the current and was gone.

Forrest and his men pursued in relays, some chasing Federals up the road to Ripley and picking up prisoners from the exhausted enemy falling down by the roadside, while others rested and ate boiled beans and bacon from the captured wagons. Forrest himself was still on the trail of Sturgis's scattered remnants when daylight picked out the party he led. There was not much of the joy of victory on his countenance.

"Why don't you look happy?" Anderson asked him. "We've had a big day."

"We ought to had all of 'm," Forrest said shortly.

"I'll say we got plenty," Nath Boon said. "And still picken up more."

Forrest's hard eyes were scanning the ground like the eyes of a hunter looking for a sign. Others of his men kept dismounting to collect discarded packs and weapons. Now and then on the roadway appeared one of those *Remember Fort Pillow* badges men had torn from their uniforms as they fled.

"I'll say one thing, them ornery ole niggers can *fight*—when they back's to the wall." Forrest shook his head, the point of his beard jerking side to side above the hard-pack of the road. "If not for them we'd have eaten up every last scrap of this army." In his mind already he was contemplating a letter to be sent to the Federal General Washburn at Memphis, a few jagged phrases which Anderson would later compose into more polite language: *All the negro troops stationed in Memphis took an oath on their knees, in the presence of Major General Hurlburt and other officers of your army, to avenge Fort Pillow, and that they would show my troops no quarter . . . a large majority of the prisoners we have captured from that command have voluntarily stated that they expected us to murder them . . . both sides acted as though neither felt safe in surrendering, even when further resistance was useless.*

While Tecumseh Sherman on the news of Brice's Crossroads would be writing to the U.S. Secretary of War . . . *Forrest is the devil, and I think he has got some of our troops under cover. I have two officers at Memphis who will fight all the time, A. J. Smith and Mower . . . I will order them to make up a force and go out to follow Forrest to the death, if it costs ten thousand lives and breaks the Treasury. There will never be peace in Tennessee until Forrest is dead . . . .*

By afternoon of the day after the battle, they were riding near the town of Salem when some of the men with Forrest remarked their general had gone to sleep in the saddle. His change of state was just barely noticeable; he still held himself straight, but a bit more limber; his eyes had closed; now and then his head rolled to one side or the other with the movement of the dapple gray horse, then righted itself but without the eyes opening.

"But someone must wake him," Anderson said.

"Go on, then," Nath Boone replied. "Help yoreself! You know he's apt to swop your head off afore he knows right well who you are."

Anderson shook his head and took no further action. They rode on, without saying anything more about Forrest's situation, until the dapple gray horse, who was also sleepwalking, blundered full on into a tree. Forrest slipped down as slack as if his clothes were empty, rolled to his back, and continued his slumber uninterrupted. Men gathered quietly under the tree and watched him as he slept.

11

LAURIE MICHAUD-KAY

Susan

She hurried the visitors out the door and reached for the key in the deadbolt. Her fingers paused, gripping the cold metal. Which did she fear confronting the most—the threat from within or the threat from without? She had planned this carefully, weighed all the options. The fear was there, but also the excitement. How many people had a chance to explore for ghosts in an expansive antebellum home, its walls imprinted with nearly one hundred fifty years of history? She might not get this chance again. She planned to move out of town, leaving her job as tour guide at the historic site. Her fingers snapped the lock into place.

She had more to fear from the living than from the dead. But her stalker couldn't possibly know that she had chosen this afternoon to stay late. He never showed up here anyway, but waited for her near the apartment, scolding her in letters for stopping somewhere on the way home, disappointing him at the minutes lost until he could see her again. No, she had time for her paranormal investigation. She took a deep breath, turned, and walked down the empty hallway.

He watched her latch the door and come toward him. He could feel her nervousness. Her name was Susan. It was what had first attracted him. His wife's name had been Susan. It was nice to think of Susan in the house again. It reminded him of the golden years after the war, when he could again control everything in his life. When Susan was alive. When he could kiss her, lie beside her in bed. As he drew further back into the shadows, his hungry whisper lingered in the air. "Susan . . ."

Susan stopped at the end of the hallway and retrieved the flashlight from behind a stack of brochures. The remaining daylight would fade to a soft darkness in the hour she expected to be in the house. She did not plan to use the lights and would switch on the flashlight only if she needed to. Ghosts liked the dark. It was a tenet of the paranormal.

But she wasn't up to roaming the antebellum house in total darkness. Besides, she had to be out before the local police did their nightly check of the property. Her car was still in the parking lot. As a guide, she had the right to be inside the house. She just didn't want to explain to them *why* she was there with no lights on.

"Okay, girl, let's go," Susan said out loud, as much to rally her courage as to spur herself on. At least she thought she had said "girl." Her ears echoed back "Susan." She couldn't be hearing things already. Ghost-hunting distorted perceptions from your eyes and ears, teased your imagination. Oddly, though, being a stalking-victim would help counteract this phenomenon. After months of vigilance, her senses were attuned to things out of the ordinary—subtle noises, abrupt shifts in atmosphere. But she had to anchor her mind in rational thought, find logical explanations for noises and sights, or the entire experiment would be invalid.

Putting it down to nerves, Susan pushed open the swinging door and entered the original portion of the two-story house. The Preservation Society had done a marvelous job in restoring the structure and interior. Most of it reflected the house as it would have been after the Civil War. Some of the furnishings were family pieces from that period. However, the Society had kept the closets, bathrooms, heating, and electric lights that had been incorporated after the turn of the century, as well as the wing she had just left, which consolidated the original kitchen and smokehouse, and now housed the Society offices and a modern kitchen.

The passage from the wing had brought Susan into the dining room. She gazed at the large oval table immediately in front of her, attuning her senses to the atmosphere of the room. Confederate generals had faced their destiny over its polished walnut surface that autumn morning in 1864. The enemy had slipped through their presumed blockade of the road in front of the house. Their boys had been exhausted after chasing Union forces as they moved north from Atlanta. Now their commander was in a rage, thumping the table repeatedly and shouting orders. Their troops would follow the Yankees to Franklin and attack in an all-out attempt to stop the bastards from getting to Nashville.

This well-known chapter in the house's history was rumored to evoke a residual haunting. Tension thickened the air, making visitors uncomfortable. People heard dishes rattling as the general's fist slammed into the table. Others swore that they actually glimpsed the heated exchange, watching and listening as the Confederates argued the strategy of a frontal assault at Franklin—shadowy figures oblivious to the passage of time, unaware of modern observers.

Susan had read that residual hauntings could be tied to a specific hour or time of year. She had chosen this late November day exactly for that reason. It was the anniversary of the historic battle. True, the breakfast had happened in the morning, and it was now twilight, but she was hopeful the spirits would react to the day, rather than the time. She waited, focusing her senses on the room.

Nothing. Susan relaxed a bit. Even the power of suggestion had failed to produce an apparition in the room. Glancing at her watch, she realized that she needed to move on if she wanted to walk through the entire house before her hour was gone.

She entered the front parlor. The portrait of the original owner hung over the fireplace. An exacting man, he had torn down the walls of the house three times before satisfied that he could safely move his wife and children into the spacious structure. They had occupied the house just five years before the Civil War started. As with most prosperous local farmers, he had been a Southern sympathizer, alarmed at the recent government actions that threatened to destroy his means of supporting this family. He organized a local infantry company and served the C.S.A. as a major. Captured twice, he spent nearly two years as a prisoner. And if the stories were true, eternity being a ghost.

Rousing herself, she decided to cover the upstairs next. She had no trouble seeing as she entered the central hall and started up the wide staircase. The evening light fell through the row of windows on the landing above. She was aware of the quiet of the empty house, heard the ticking of the clock in the parlor. Suddenly, she heard a brief, familiar creak of door hinges. Her hand gripped the stair rail. It was the noise made by the swinging door when she pushed it open to lead her tour group into the main house. Was it the police, come earlier than usual? She hadn't heard their car, but it was hard to hear outside noises through the twenty-inch brick walls. No footsteps. Oh, God. It couldn't be him. Her stalker had taken pains to demonstrate that he was skilled in stealth. He taunted her in letters with intimate details of her home life that he had secretly observed, comparing this activity to his covert war ops. He bragged that he had only been stopped once, on an overseas mission that had been bungled. He had been captured and held as a POW. The internment had stung his pride, and after being liberated, he had trained so that he would not be captured again. No one could stop him from being with her.

Was he here?

Susan turned on the stair, aiming the flashlight, her thumb ready on the switch. Then she shook her head. The noise could not possibly have come from the swinging door. It had a stout, old-fashioned sliding bolt that she had locked in place after entering the dining room. No one could move that door when the bolt was in place. A group of teenagers had tried it after breaking into the offices one night. They had jimmied and hammered on the door, but it never budged.

Reassured by her logic, Susan turned and continued up the stairs. As she passed the landing windows, she glanced outside. Her car was the only one in the parking lot.

He could hear her moving slowly from one room to another. Occasionally, he heard her voice. She was always talking to herself, he knew. Her progress was easy to follow as the wood floors creaked overhead. He would wait for her down here, in the chair by the fireplace. Susan must finish her chores . . . take care of the house . . . before they could be in each other's company. But he would see her from the moment she descended the lower portion of the stairs. He sighed in anticipation, leaning back into the soft cushions. So different from the hard, filthy surfaces of the prison camp. Deprivation heightened your appreciation of the comforts of home, he mused. He looked around the room, noting the placement of the furniture in the shadowy edges of the room. The silken settee, a maple floor clock, the spinet desk placed under the window overlooking the garden. The hall end table, the fringe on its embroidered scarf gently moving. The side door must be slightly ajar, letting in a telltale current of air. He started to get up and then realized Susan was moving toward the stairs. Lovely Susan. Deprivation certainly heightened your appreciation of that, as well. He settled back in the chair.

Susan's footsteps resonated on the bare floor as she moved toward the stairs. She had wandered through each room, poking into the closets and cupboards, lightly touching period keepsakes, listening beside beds. She had stepped onto the back balcony, envisioning a thriving plantation, where crops of wheat, corn, and cotton grew in the nearby fields, and slaughtered hogs were laid out behind the smokehouse in preparation for dressing and salt-curing.

She had spent the most time in the second-floor kitchen. A figure had been seen in the window of this room by other staff members, always when the house was empty. She had tried to provoke an intelligent haunting by politely introducing herself and asking its reasons for haunting the home. She went so far as to demand a sign of its presence. As if in answer, the windows had rattled slightly and a distant clanking noise could be heard. With a whoosh, the heating system announced its presence . . . but nothing else. She was proud to have maintained her objectivity in the face of the house's dark corners and night sounds, and a tad disappointed. It was time to check out the remaining rooms downstairs and leave.

The row of windows glowed softly from the floodlights now illuminating the exterior. Stepping onto the landing, Susan was startled by her long shadow stretching across the hall floor below. Uneasiness surged through her. The atmosphere grew tense, charged. Her objectivity faltered as her eyes moved to the dark entrances on either side of the hall. Her primal sense took control, whispering danger. Her heartbeat accelerated. Something was in the shadows below.

He could see her on the landing, an angel surrounded by a soft light. Susan. She was finally coming to be with him. She would sit in the delicate chair opposite him. They would talk about the future. Then they would retire for the night. He leaned forward. What was she waiting for? Why did she suddenly seem frozen, a look of fear on her face? He was puzzled and now slightly out of humor. Why was she keeping him waiting? What was this foolishness? A whisper reached him, and he realized with a jolt that his feelings were echoed by another person in the room, a person hidden behind him, waiting in the darkness. No, not echoed. These feelings were coiled, depraved, and threatening, ready to be unleashed.

Susan heard the scream just as she turned to run. It reverberated with human agony and seemed to go on during the seconds she was fleeing to the second floor kitchen. There was a fire escape off the room. She was no longer driven by logic or objectivity. Terror had taken over. Just as she reached the window, she heard the side door slam back against the wall. She saw someone stumbling through the garden. He continually turned to look back, as if terrified that he was being followed. She recognized his face in the security lights.

It was her stalker.

Suddenly he froze, his staring eyes locked on the house. He crouched down, covering his head with his arms. His second scream was cut off as a shadow seemed to move over him. Then he jumped up and tore for the woods. This time he did not look back. He disappeared into the trees, only to reappear seconds later, the headlights of his car bouncing across the uneven ground in a desperate effort to get his spinning tires to cover the distance more quickly.

"What the . . ." Susan muttered, her own uncontrolled terror broken by the sight of the man's frantic retreat. She shivered, feeling a trace of cold air behind her. She turned, her eyes trying to penetrate the shadows in the room. It was quiet again, but colder. The night air must be blowing through the open side door. She felt the need to close it, to stop the cold and her own reactionary shaking. But this was no time for taking chances. Whatever had caused the man to flee might still be downstairs. She pulled out her cell phone and called the police.

After reporting a break-in, Susan listened again. There

were no footsteps, no creaking floorboards. But the cold was becoming unbearable. She started quietly for the stairs. Hoping for the advantage, she switched on the chandelier when she reached the landing. The lower hall flooded with light. Blinking in the brilliance, she paused, assessing the atmosphere. The paralyzing knowledge of a presence was gone, even though the rooms off the hall were not completely lit. She was alone again in the house.

She could hear the reassuring sound of the police siren in the distance as she hurried down the remaining steps and across to the open side door. Standing in its shadow, she stared into the garden. There had been terror on his face. Whatever happened to him, he deserved it. She shut the door and walked into the parlor to wait for the police.

The sight of him knocked the breath out of her. He stood in front of the fireplace, watching her face. He was older than in the portrait behind him, his whiskers grayer, his hair sparser, his face lined from the months spent in the Union prison camp.

Susan knew that she should be frightened, but instead a feeling of love and safety settled over her. He came to her and looked into her eyes. His voice, deep and soothing, resonated in her mind.

"He'll never bother you again, my dear. I've seen to that."

Susan was still staring at the empty spot when the police came into the room.

ROBERT HICKS

I Think I Attract the Mentally Ill

"**N**onsense!" she said. "It's the bookstores that draw them in. They go there because they have no other place to go. Bookstores are warm and well lit and safe. They're comforting. If I was mentally ill and had been thrown out of some state facility, I'd go to a bookstore, too." Then she added, "I'm sure that Nicholas Sparks has the same problem when he's doing in-store events."

Her feeble attempt to reassure me only helped reinforce my long-held suspicion. I began to envision a store full of women screaming, snapping pictures, and throwing underwear at Nicholas Sparks. They were hanging on his every word. They loved every moment he afforded them away from their far-duller lives without him. If these fans could be called mentally ill, it was some mild universal form of illness born out of solitary loneliness or, even worse, being married to men who really didn't know them.

Nicholas Sparks offered comfort, as his protagonists always suffered the loss of love, only to find a deeper, richer love and fulfillment by the end of each book. Who wouldn't want to believe that if her disinterested husband or boyfriend were to die, there would be a richer, better life waiting in the wings with someone who not only listened, but who cared?

As much as I truly wanted to believe my editor, nothing she said could remove the gnawing sense from within that seemed to say I had been singled out by the deranged for special treatment.

Maybe she was right, that the stores were providing the perfect Petri dish for the broken masses. Yet, there seemed to be more to it than just that. After all, I had written about an emotionally fragile woman who re-interred the dead and created a cemetery in her backyard. And it was about the Civil War. For Pete's sake, if I didn't want to attract the fringe, what was I thinking?

No, the truth was there before me from that first event at my local bookstore, when two clearly problemed devotees of a book they had never read—a man and a woman—got in a slugfest over who would be last to meet me, and the woman won. Somehow in the commotion, as the staff was ushering me out a side door, I knew in my heart that this was going to be a long book tour.

They seemed to come out of thin air. What should have been ordinary, run-of-the-mill book events, were turned into three-ring circuses before the watching world. The craziest fans always wanted to be last in line, wanted to kidnap my attention. Understand, I'm not talking about the regular folks who stood in line to tell me about an ancestor who fought in the Civil War. They were fine—good, solid folks who simply loved history or "their people" or the history of "their people." There can be no complaint with them.

No, I am talking about the other ones, the ones who had "special messages" for me. Messages that no one else could hear, that had to be delivered in whispers. They were the ones who would come up behind me while I was signing books and lay hands on my shoulders and start praying in tongues. Or there was the lady who spread out naked pictures of herself, reminding me that most folks should best keep their clothes on. Let's just say, I'm betting Nick Sparks gets better naked pictures.

There were the ones who would shake my hand when I signed their book, but, somehow, forget to release it. They followed me to my car, gushing stories about really nothing. They often spoke about leaving their lives behind and traveling with me on the tour or holding a séance to retrieve the dead I had written about.

The dead—above all, there were the dead. The kid from *The Sixth Sense* had nothing on me. Oh, maybe the fact that he could actually see them puts him in another league, but according to my following, the dead surround me at every turn.

The first time someone mentioned the dead—who would soon seem to crowd out every bookstore event—I jokingly replied that it was regrettable so few of them still bought books. I quickly learned not to joke about the dead. Don't get me wrong. The dead never seemed to bear offense, or if they did, they kept it to themselves. No, it was only the living, the ones with their "special messages" for me, who seemed to have misplaced their sense of humor in the same spot where they had left their minds.

Somehow, as she groaned on about Nick Sparks, I realized my editor was not getting the picture. Nick Sparks' problems, if he had any, were no doubt fueled by his devotees' libido. I should be so lucky. Naked pictures of folks, who should have had the decency to keep their clothes on, are not like a discrete pair of panties in my hand as I sign a book. Nor were there messages to meet up afterward at my hotel's bar. Like I said, most of the messages I got were from the dead.

Then again, maybe she was right. Maybe I had blown it all up. After all, I am a fiction writer. Point was, I needed to relax and enjoy those folks who took the time to come to store events, buy my book, and pray over me in tongues.

So we headed out to a signing for the paperback at a big chain store on the Upper West Side. Fortunately, in that neighborhood, there should be a good-sized gathering of Southerners who had gone north to seek fortune, but who still clung to their roots. But, then again, this was New York, and there should be a healthy-sized crowd of unhealthy folks.

By the time we arrived, the crowd numbered around sixty, and, sure enough, it was populated by a lot of Southerners. They were the ones wearing oxford cloth or plaid flannel shirts with khaki pants in November. They seemed comfortable in their clothes and manners. It was good that I was wrong. My editor needed to see that I could draw a good crowd of interested, educated readers.

Once it began, the event seemed to flow along with ease. After so many of these in-stores, I could do them in my sleep. Like anyone before an audience, I fed off their good wishes, and the event went well. That is, until I opened it up for Q & A.

From out of nowhere, a guy with the best Rastafarian hair I had ever seen on a white guy—part Jamaican, part Sideshow Bob—raised his hand. When I acknowledged him, he said he had a two-part question for me. He asked that I wait until he had finished asking both questions to answer them.

From the moment he opened his mouth, I knew this was not a two-part question, this was an assassination. His first question was whether I believed in reincarnation. I was numb as I stood there waiting for his next shot. From the dress of the crowd, it was clear that the room had its fair share of duck hunters, and I was this guy's duck.

He asked me if I had been killed at the Battle of Franklin.

I paused until he asked me to answer the first question. I said, no, I didn't believe in reincarnation. With that, he lunged from his seat and shrieked, "Well, I guess we have your answer to my second question, don't we?"

I nodded and then turned to the audience and asked if they had any other questions about my book. My new friend was not to be ignored. Still standing in the middle of the special-events area, he bellowed, "What would you say if I told you I was killed in Da Nang, Vietnam, on April 24, 1968?"

Why did I do it? I'll go to my grave asking myself why. For,

I THINK I ATTRACT THE MENTALLY ILL

without pause, I turned and replied, "Cool!" I know it wasn't the right response, but sometimes there is no other answer from someone of my generation.

He screamed back, "It wasn't cool, buddy! I bled for over four hours until I finally pumped out every ounce in me and died. I can remember my body growing cold, yet the wracking pain only ending in my death. I was buried at Arlington with full honors, and all you can say is 'Cool!' What kind of sick person are you?"

At that moment I was offered the opportunity to take the high road and humbly apologize, but I didn't.

I waited for him to catch his breath and replied that, as a Southerner, there was a uniquely Southern way to use the word "cool." Often, I added, Southerners used the word "cool" in response to a great tragedy like "Your mother just died!" or "The world is coming to an end!" and I tried to ignore the puzzled looks on the faces of the Southerners in the audience. Maybe my response would fly and we could move on. But, no, my new friend was not going to give me even this, and he raged, "I don't believe you!"

Now we were at war, my dead, reincarnated, mentally ill friend and me. I asked how many folks in the gathering were Southerners, to which maybe twenty or so timidly raised their hands. I asked them, wasn't it true that often, as Southerners, they had responded to shockingly bad news with "cool"? At that moment not one of them wanted to be there. Hell, none of us wanted to be there. But I wasn't backing away and I was taking every one of my fellow Southerners with me. Reluctantly they joined in my big lie and sheepishly nodded yes. I had won. I had silenced the crazy one for good. Victory was sweet.

Now, regaining control of the room, I asked if anyone had one last question. Before anyone could even think of a question to ask, Sideshow Bob jumped back up and asked if he could ask just one more question.

Without waiting for permission, he asked, "Do you know who killed JFK?"

I took a deep breath and without thinking I replied, "Yes."

With longing earnestness he asked, "Who?"

I sized him up as I took my next breath and said, "I'm not telling."

The event ended and the bookstore folks ushered him away. I signed books and listened attentively to folks telling me about their ancestors who fought in the Civil War.

My editor quietly waited for me with my overcoat in hand. We left the store after thanking the staff for their help. As we made our way down the street, she said, "I may have been wrong. Maybe you're really not attracting Nick Sparks' crowd."

CARROLL CHAMBERS MOTH

For the Respect of Family and Friends

Mama said Daddy woulda been different if our lives warnt so hard. All Daddy ever wanted was to own his own land, grow his own crops, and get his own mule to plow his plot. That's what he needed for the respect of his family and friends.

It was a hardscrabble life in the 30s, and not only cause of the Depression. Heck, we had a few rich people to live in town, but we didn't mix with them. We kept to ourselves. We knowed the rules. We knowed folk down on their luck, but in our neck of the woods, we was always down on our luck. If it warnt the crops failin, it was the weather or sickness or the shine.

On a really bad night like tonight, Mama would say, "James, you was born on a night like this." So I guess that's why I always think of Mama when the rain pounds the tin roof. I can still see Mama sittin in her chair shuckin corn or snappin beans, dressed in some kind of pink outfit.

My mama was a good woman, simple in her ways and hard workin. Anybody in need, she'd be there. She woulda slept with her Bible under her pillow if she could. She did her best to be good to us younguns, too, not in worldly ways, but with praise, and a go at the switch sometime. "Spare the rod, spoil the child," she'd say, but it was more the threat that worked. When Mama died, she musta gone straight to heaven. I truly believe this, cause she had to endure my daddy.

Daddy and Mama met the summer she was sixteen and she come to town to visit a friend. Daddy had just enough sense and shine in him to ask a pretty girl in a pink dress to dance. I always thought that was why Mama wore pink, just to please Daddy. Mama said Daddy was different then. He laughed more. Without the moonshine he didn't talk too much. Accordin to Mama, they got married, went to the picture show for their honeymoon, and shared a box of Good n Plenty to celebrate. They rented a small plot of land, and for a short time life was real good—even with them so young and poor and all.

In time there was five of us—Mama, Daddy, Johnny, Billy Joe, and me. Mama had three other babies but they was born still. They was between Billy Joe and me. Mama always loved her babies, but she could only have three. Daddy wanted more. That way, he'd have more help on the farm. He was disappointed, but he kept workin the land, thinkin of the mule he wanted.

Mama growed flowers, mostly pinks, purples, and reds. She tended a garden—tomatoes, butterbeans, okra, sweet potatoes, and snap beans. Watermelons, too. My brothers and me picked blackberries that growed along the fence by the road. For a short while we had a few chickens till the snakes got the eggs and the fox got the chickens. Daddy raised a little patch of corn and always managed to get some of it in a pot on the fire mixed with sugar and water. In time both the corn and Daddy got brewed.

Furniture in our house was sparse, but Mama made it cozy. One full pink dress became curtains. Then Daddy almost set he place afire makin his brew. Mama told him to move his pot outside.

My brothers and me had a good life on our place. We had full run of the land after chores.

Sometimes Mr. Bledsoe and Mr. Cleveland would come over, and Daddy and them would set down and have a drink.

They'd jaw bout most anything—the cotton crop, mostly. Sometimes they brought their wives, and then Mama and them would talk quilts and rainfall and the neighbors' business. Sometimes the families got together and brought food, and we had a lot to eat then. Those was good times.

By the time Johnny was thirteen, Billy Joe was twelve, and I was eight, Daddy was workin longer hours, his eye still on the mule. He was plowin all by hisself with no mule in sight. Weather and general bad luck gave us losses. I remember one summer was so hot, we had no rain for over a month. Animals was dyin in the fields. There warnt enough hay, and wasps come after us just to get their thirst filled.

Most folk we knowed didn't wear shoes in summer. We went barefoot and our feet grew larger. As the air got cooler, we wore hand-me-downs or hand-me-ups, as the case may be. Some folk only had one large pair of shoes, and whoever had to go to town got to put on the shoes. If the shoes was too small, you got blisters. If they was too large, you got a pebble inside. We went to school and did chores, and when the winter rains fell, we was wearin old cloth shoes Mama got from some missionary ladies. The shoes got cold and wet. We'd pack em with paper or rags and put em near the fire to dry. When they dried out, they was tight . . . as tight as Daddy's face. Mama was wearin her pink dresses, but they was old and faded now. Daddy didn't notice. He was wearin frustration.

The only thing that was increasin was the size of the corn brew pot.

When Daddy's friends come and set down, they'd fun Daddy bout the crops and ask him when he'd be gettin the mule. Then they'd have another drink.

Sometimes we'd get Daddy to take us huntin for rabbit or squirrel. Mama wouldn't fix possum. She said possums was scavengers. We didn't know what that meant, but it warnt good. We learnt to read Mama's face. Fishin for bream or catfish was good fun, too, and Mama didn't have a "look" for a catch of fish. Those was the best times we ever had. I loved my daddy as much as my mama did. Maybe more. We had good times together and we'd laugh if Daddy warnt drinkin. If he thought we crossed him when he was drinkin, he'd never hit us, but he'd say, "I brought you into this world and I kin take you out," and he got this strange look in his eye—a look that made you wonder what kind of creature he was. Somethin like the look a trapped animal gets.

I saw that look one night when Cleveland and Bledsoe was over. Again they was funnin Daddy. Cleveland said, "So, how come Foster kin git a mule and you caint? He don't have three boys like you, and he got hisself a mule. He done sold so many crops, he bought another piece of land." Bledsoe said, "Yeah, you gonna let some colored man buy up another plot while you still dreamin of a mule someday?"

My daddy smiled with his mouth but not with his eyes.

Daddy was different after that night, even with Mama. The light just went out of him. We rarely went huntin and stopped fishin, but Cleveland and Bledsoe still showed up to set and jaw. We could never understand why they enjoyed windin up Daddy so.

I heard from Johnny that somethin happened to Foster's mule. It was found dead with a single shot through its head, and rumor was that Foster was seen leavin the farm—leavin for good, some folk said. Musta been true, cause we never seen him after that.

One night Cleveland and Bledsoe showed up to see Daddy. They talked bout Foster's trouble. Daddy looked at the floor but said nothin. Then he looked sideways at me, sort of ashamed. We both knew. Foster was never spoke of in our house again.

Somethin happened that night inside me. As I sit now listenin to the rain, I remember: it was then that I decided that when I growed up and got my own plot of land, I'd never let my daddy near my mules.

14

MADISON PERCY JONES

Sim Denny

The death of Earl Banks had consequences that went beyond the near-riot it caused and the bitter feeling that lingered for a long time in Okaloosa's black community. One of the people affected, in a different way, was Sim Denny.

Sim Denny was a Negro with skin about the color of an eggplant. He was a tall man though stooped a little now, after sixty-six years of which at least fifty had been years of hard work. It was not just the years that had bent him, though. Partly it was a shortness of breath that had come on him: it seemed he could breathe easier when he bent over a little. His heart, he reckoned, and did not inquire any further. He just went a bit slower at his job of cement finisher and occasionally thought about hiring a helper to take some of the load off of him. He had used to employ two helpers. But that was before his wife died, six years ago, and before everything got so different. Since then, working, and being, alone had got to be a habit. It was a hard habit to break, even when finally his lonesomeness began to frighten him.

Sim had never been very talkative but there had not been any reason except that he was quiet by nature. When there started to be another reason to keep quiet, he hardly even minded, at first. He went on with his cement finishing, working almost always for white people, proud when he pleased them and made them acknowledge his mastery, the finish like glass he could put on a cement surface. He went on showing respect, even when he did not feel it, saying Yas Sah to them—Yas Sah this and Yas Sah that. And he went on making three or four visits a year, for old time's sake, to the home of Mr. Will Cottrell over there in the hill section where the class white folks lived. In those days Sim did not mind a bit breaking his accustomed quiet to give a piece of his mind to offending black people. "What you want go to school with them for?" he would say. "Ain't black folks good enough for you?" Or, "You behave yoself, they treat you awright." And that first march, about the schools, had made him sneer. "Crazy niggers. Making trouble for ev'ybody."

That was how it went, back then. Sim was the aggressor and half the people he confronted like this were silent in ways that meant they agreed with him. Soon, though, there were not so many. In time there were almost none at all, or none who would admit it. That was when his remarks began to be answered not with silences anymore but with open scorn and ridicule. There were some people who now called him, right to his face, Uncle Tom or Rastus or White Man's Nigger. Even his own daughter Maybelle sometimes did, though this was mostly because of her husband.

They lived in Sim's house, in the Creektown district of Okaloosa. It was a nice house, small but of clean sound white-painted frame, on a street where now the rest of the houses resembled beehives made of red brick. In back of the house was a little outbuilding where Sim had used to keep his tools but where, nowadays, he spent most of his time when he was at home, sleeping on a cot he had put there. There were two big shade trees, a black oak and a chinaberry, and between the house and the street a decent stretch of yard that Sim, until lately, had always insisted be kept swept bare. Just like a nigger. That was what Maybelle had said to him, more than once, quoting her husband, Herman. From the very first Sim had been more than half afraid of Herman.

It was not so much a physical fear, though there was some of that. Herman had bad light eyes and an ugly razor scar like a worm on his neck. He was not big, he was just too quick. He moved around like a nervous cat, especially when he was angry, and he seemed to be always angry, seething. But Sim might have lived with this. What made him really afraid was something else about Herman. He could see it reflected—more than a reflection—in his own daughter, who had gone off to Birmingham one kind of a girl and come back another kind, pretty near as much of a stranger as that one she brought with her. Right here was the trouble, though. All of a sudden it was like Sim was the stranger, in his own house. Maybelle said things to him, hushed him up. Herman with those bad light eyes just looked at him. Then there started to be meetings in Sim's house, people he had known since they were children who looked at him now almost the way Herman did, as if Sim was something between a joke and a threat. Things he heard said in his own house gave the same kind of hitch to his breathing that hard work did sometimes. By now Sim had all but stopped saying the kind of things he used to say.

He moved out, into the toolhouse. "It make a fine room," he said to Maybelle. "Mo private. Won't be no bother to you."

"You don't have to." Maybelle's underlip was out, purple-looking, and her voice was flat. "This here yo house."

It did not seem like it. "It's awright," he said. "Make a fine room."

"We be out of here fo long." She kept on mopping the floor, with long hard thrusts of the mop. "Soon's Herman make them white people at the mill pay him mo money."

Once Sim would have said, "It's plenty good jobs for maids you could get." Now he said, "It's awright. You welcome here."

It was all right in the toolhouse, with his bed and cabinet and chairs and his wife's picture on the board wall. Except at breakfast and supper he rarely had to see Herman at all and he could not hear the voices when the meetings took place in the house. It seemed like his thoughts went better too, as if they had got almost free of spying eyes. He could drop back unseen to his childhood days on old Mr. Will Cottrell's farm, to young Mr. Will and himself, naked as a pair of snakes, diving off the sycamore tree into the blue creek pool. And the billy goat Sam they used to bait, making him hit the fence like a cannonball. Riding on top of the cotton wagons, deep in cotton, on gold late October afternoons. Mr. Will. Months since Sim had gone to visit, to sit on the back stoop or in the kitchen with him and call up those old things and talk about these new times and shake their heads and have a drink together. Lean Mr. Will now, rheumy in his eyes. And months had gone by. This thought was like a heavy weight riding on Sim's chest.

There was another weight riding on him, one that was more constant and growing heavier week by week. There were times when he felt like somebody in enemy country, a spy who people knew was a spy and who, since he was not a very dangerous one, they simply let be. At the start of that big mess about the schools, when the black people made that first march up to City Hall, Sim had watched from the sidewalk and sneered and said things to the people around him. When almost a year later the second march happened he watched it too, but in silence now, the sneer locked up in his breast. Standing mute on the sidewalk with a little space between him and the others, he watched, knowing many or most of the marchers, the sullen black faces passing by in ranks, and watched their mouths stretch open when they started to sing like they were walking into a church about how they were going to overcome. Overcome. He shook his head. It was a gesture nobody noticed. He went home feeling lonely.

That was the same week when Sim decided he would not go to church anymore, not until they stopped all that and got back to the Bible. He stuck to it. Sunday mornings he slept and read his Bible and let his mind drop back, dreaming. He began to work harder at his job, even if it did make his breath come short, and down on his knees stroking wide with his float he put finishes on cement floors that a person could see his face in. Then winter came on, a wet winter with skies dripping all the time and the earth a slush to walk on and there was not much work for him. Most of the day he was in his little room out back and when he did not turn on his lamp the light was like a desolate leaded-colored pall. That was when Sim started to be afraid.

His dreams seemed to be the cause. He was now in the habit of lying on his bed and, between sleeping and waking, letting his mind drop back to the old time, the childhood time. But so often now something would happen that he could not control. Suddenly, back there in the middle of one of those bright memories, he would look around and not be able to find Mr. Will, no matter how hard he looked—or anybody else either. He would be, maybe, out in the big pasture behind the house and, looking around for Mr. Will, discover also that the house was gone and the land was not green anymore and the sky gave no light except this desolate leaden one. It was a winter place, without any motion or voices or any landmark to guide him out of it.

Sim thought it would be better when spring came and sunlight and hard work again. But the bad weather kept on into April and then, when May came, that first strangling happened. The event did not seem at first to mean anything special for Sim. An old white lady strangled in her home on the other side of town: Mrs. Rosa Callahan. Sim had known the family long ago. He silently shook his head. Such a time. But there was more to it than he had foreseen. Within a few days there was a tale, a rumor going around. Sim was late to hear it. People, even Maybelle, did not tell him things anymore and because Herman had been absent for a couple of days there had been no talk at the supper table for Herman to listen in on. So the rumor was already at full flower on the night Sim first heard Herman talking in his bitterest voice to Maybelle about it.

"Nigger hair. Yeah. They knows nigger hair when they sees it . . . ev'y time. Yeah."

Afraid to ask, afraid of drawing Herman's anger, Sim had to listen a while before he could get it straight. Hair. They had found it under one of the dead lady's fingernails: black hair, nigger hair. So it was a black man that had done it to her. Bent over his plate Sim kept on making his hand lift the food to his mouth.

"So a nigger done it. That's all they need, a little black hair. If it's bad, a nigger done it."

Without looking Sim could see those light eyes on fire. He could actually see, obliquely, Herman's knotted brown hand holding the dinner fork as if for a weapon, making it shimmer under the bright light bulb.

"Got to get 'em one, now. They be down here to get 'em one. Anybody do fine. Might be me."

Bowed, Sim kept working his jaw. Then he felt the eyes and suddenly could not swallow what he had chewed.

"Won't be you, Uncle. You got white folks. They takes care of *their* niggers."

"Lay off him," Maybelle said, but not with much force.

Sim managed to swallow the food but he could not meet the eyes, the anger coming straight at him.

"He one of their pets. He ain't got no worries."

"Ain't nobody's pet," Sim said gruffly.

"Lay off him, Herman," Maybelle said.

Herman withdrew his gaze, let it pass carelessly across Maybelle's face and settle on his half-eaten plate of food. He speared a carrot with the fork. "All the same, I wouldn't feel easy if Uncle thought *I* was the one done it."

Sim drew a breath, drew hard to fill his lungs. "Ain't nobody's pet. I'm a black man same as you."

Herman bit off the carrot. Chewing, he said, "On the outside, awright. But just only yo hide, is all." Still chewing, he got up from the table and went into the living room and then out the front door, letting the screen bang shut.

"Eat yo supper now, Daddy."

He could not eat. He pretended to, hiding the crisis of breath that had come on him, until it was possible to escape.

The next Sunday, after more than six months, Sim went to church. Somebody was there already sitting in the place up front that used to be always saved for him and he had to sit near the back close under the white-painted wall where hung the picture of Jesus making the waters be still. It was like Sim was not noticed, had not even been missed. His nods and his smiles drew nothing but the slightest kind of answers and he sat there under the picture feeling like somebody invisible, too still to be noticed. When the singing swelled he tried to join in but his breath was short. It seemed like the River Jordan was rolling over his head. When Brother Dick in the pulpit got going, lacing the Pharisees and the Sadducees and the white people all at once, with his voice coming like waves cresting and breaking and his strong young spade-like hands shaping out the rhythm of it; when the groans and the Amens started and the heads began to pitch and sway as if a big wind was blowing through the church; then Sim felt like somebody struck dumb and stiff and cold, unable even to stir in his pew. He kept trying, as if it was a tight shell of ice he had to break, to shatter. Finally he could move his head and then his lips and could shape the word Amen and utter it. The word came out wrong, off-key, missing the beat of things—like a tune he had failed to catch. He did not risk another try. He nodded his head, moved his lips, and hoped it would be enough for the eyes around him.

That was Sim's first effort to get back in and in a way the result frightened him more than any of his dreams had. This setback only drove him the harder, though. He not only kept on going to church, he also began to make efforts in other directions. For one thing he hired a boy, Tod Nells, to help him with his cement finishing. For another he changed his manner with white people.

Or he tried to, for he only succeeded in part: his old nigger courtesy would too often come back on him, defeating the impression he meant to give. Still there were unexpected things he said and expected things he did not say that put a look of surprise on the white faces. It was pain for him, but with Tod behind him he stood it. Also he was not so scrupulous about his work now. In fact, on purpose he would sometimes leave a whorl or a nick in a cement floor and then turn sullen if there was a complaint. Shoddy work was pain too, though. He had moments in his room when it felt as if those whorls and nicks were graven on his soul.

It seemed when it was black people Sim talked to that he could not say those things rightly. Always there was that note like a cracked bell, ringing false. It was not only too plain to him, it also made people's eyes look at him with second sight. His one and only try with Herman, a remark about "Whitey" he had overheard somewhere, brought that look and more besides into Herman's face. "Look out now, Uncle," he said, showing his yellow teeth. "What yo white folks gon think about that kind of talk?" Sim learned not to say those things except when he had to and then he studied about each one, figured how to say it. Most of the time he settled for just agreeing with what he heard said, nodding, and poking his lip out.

They did not believe him, though. It did not seem to matter how often he went to church or how many people he nodded his agreement with or how painfully rude he made himself act with white people sometimes. Because it was an act. You had to be what you pretended or people saw through it, heard it in your voice. To say a thing right you had to be it. And this meant you had to give up things. Like Mr. Will, thinking about him. Like letting your mind drop back, too. Now Sim tried not to think about those old things anymore. And finally he got another idea. But that was not till September, after that fifth white woman got strangled and the police killed poor old deaf and dumb Earl Banks for it.

The night after that happened there was a big meeting outside the Baptist Church, with people crowded in the churchyard and the whole street too, singing, and Brother Dick and Hershel Rawls on the church steps shouting and praying and waving their arms. Some gangs of black boys went uptown on Cotton Street and broke windows and yelled at the police and got, a lot of them, put in jail. The day after that there was a march, to City Hall, and a meeting on the steps between the mayor and Hershel Rawls. In those days Creektown was like a place on fire, except there were not any flames or smoke. The nights were noisy, broken with sudden outcries and cars going by faster than usual and people talking in the streets. Nobody talked about anything else. And Sim was afraid.

It was, when he could think clearly about it, not a fear that any personal violence might be done to him. And yet to make himself come out of his little room in the backyard was all Sim's strength could manage. It was as if outside there were howling winds with fierce eddies that would seize and twist his body and cruelly wrench his limbs out of their sockets. He lay on his bed straining for breath. And yet he went out. He was at the meeting at the church that night. The next day with everybody else he marched to City Hall and stood there in the crowd, standing so far back that he could see nothing except, now and then, the bald head of the mayor and the agitated black one of Hershel Rawls. Of what they were saying, of their voices even, he could not hear anything. What were they saying, talking about? Suddenly, like a dream coming on, he could not even imagine what, any more than he could think why he and all this listening murmurous crowd of black people were standing here in the town square in the harsh sun of early September. But that moment grew from dream to nightmare, in which it seemed to him that he stood here alone of all this crowd in helpless ignorance, among all these black heads filled with a knowledge he could not even conceive of and that he would have given everything he had in the world to share. The sweat ran down his body, his breath came hard. His head was as light as an empty shell set on top of his neck.

But out of that terrified and confused moment Sim got his idea. He had a savings account at the bank that came to over fourteen hundred dollars. He had been building it for a good many years, putting in a little bit almost every month, and once it got past a thousand it began to be a considerable thing in his mind. He read his statements every month and thought about the money lying there in one big pile that nobody but him could lay a hand on. He had no idea of spending it, ever, he meant to leave it. There was a sort of awe in the thought of a man, a colored man anyway, having that much money to leave behind him when he died. The thought he had in bed that night after the march was still more awesome: it left him stunned. By morning, though, he had made up his mind to it and he was uptown waiting outside the door of the bank at least an hour before opening time.

That was such a day. Leaving the bank with that sealed envelope full of green money clutched tight in his hand he walked as he had used to walk thirty years ago—straight-up, long-stepping, with easy breaths of the morning air swelling, gorging his chest. Walked better in fact, as if he had grown taller and need not look any way but down into the black faces he greeted along the way. Up Cotton Street and across, ignoring traffic, down Willow Street to Bean and into Creektown he never once broke his stride or felt one lapse of this new power trilling in his blood. Children watched him as if they knew, could see it, and so, now, did the men and the women he passed by. He slowed his steps to savor it. Even so he got there too soon and, to let it build, he paused for a minute or two outside the door. It was a rectangular brick building, once a grocery, and a sign on the wall said:

OKALOOSA IMPROVEMENT ASSOCIATION.

It did not go as Sim expected, all complete in one triumphant stroke. Hershel Rawls was not there. A secretary in the small front office, in front of a shut door with a glass pane you could not see through, told him to try again in an hour. He would not state his business. He went outside and paced the street and never for long let his eyes wander from the front of that building. He was not at all crestfallen, not yet. The envelope full of green money went on ticking away like something alive between his tight thumb and fingers. An hour would make it better, the greater for being put off. The astonished smile, the welcome, on Hershel Rawls' stern face.

Sim was not to see it, though. Every hour when like clockwork he entered the building again he was met with just such another disappointment. One time, when he went in right at noon, he had thought it was about to happen for sure, because the woman told him Hershel Rawls was back there, in conference, behind that pane of glass you could not see through. But he never came out. There must have been a back door and Hershel Rawls came and went by it. At five o'clock when the whistle blew and Sim walked out of the building for the eighth and last time he felt almost as if the whole thing had been spoiled. He had not wanted to do what he finally did. It was that woman's impatience, wanting to know his business, and her face nearly as light as a white woman's. She got it out of him finally and got the envelope out of his hand. He stopped her from dropping it into a box that was there. "You give hit to him, yoself. You tell him who. You tell him Sim Denny."

She said she would, not to worry, and gave him a smile that reassured him a little.

"He got a surprise coming. When you gon give hit to him?"

She said maybe even tonight, if she saw him. Then she said, "And I know he'll be wanting to get in touch with you, to thank you."

That was most of the comfort Sim took home with him that evening. Hershel Rawls would get in touch with him, to thank him. He would send for him, or maybe even come by the house, come out back to Sim's room. And anyhow there would be that smile when he opened Sim's envelope. This thought kept coming back and growing in Sim's mind, shading out his long day's disappointment. By suppertime it had raised him almost to the pitch of this morning's elation.

He was too full to eat but he ate a little, waiting for his moment. He would have liked, to launch him, some little break in the silence over the table. But it did not come, forbidden by Herman's sullen face, his look as if it was anger alone that drove him at his food. Tonight, though, this was not enough, not for Sim. He said, "Old Hershel Rawls got him a surprise coming."

"What you talkin bout?" Maybelle said. Herman went on eating.

"When he op'm that *en*velope I left for him." Sim looked straight ahead of him at the green plaster wall.

"What *en*velope? What you talking bout?"

"That'n I left for him." He paused. "Got foteen hundert and twenty-seb'm dollar in it."

Even Herman stopped eating. Maybelle said, "Of *yo* money?"

"Ev'y penny."

It took Maybelle a moment, with her mouth open, to digest the fact. "You done gone crazy?"

"For the Mov*em*ent," Sim said. "Hershel Rawls be in touch with me." He put a bite of something in his mouth, started chewing. His head felt light with triumph.

"You gone plumb ravin crazy," Maybelle said.

"Naw." This was Herman. His bad light eyes were looking at Maybelle. "He just think he can buy his self black." Now he was looking at Sim. "Ain't that right, Uncle?"

At first somehow this shot was more confusing than painful to Sim. All he could think to say was, "I ain't 'Uncle.' "

Herman made a small derisive noise with his tongue. "Come on, Uncle. What you care bout the Mov*em*ent? Yo white folks is what you care bout." Herman suddenly put his head back.

"Hey, wait a minute." He got up and stepped through the living room door and came back immediately with a letter. "From yo white folks, Uncle." He placed it on the table beside Sim's plate.

It was hard to see but Sim could see this much—in print up in the left-hand corner. William Cottrell. And Sim's own name in the middle, shakily written with ink. He could do nothing but stare at the letter.

"Better open it. He might need you to come shine his shoes."

"Don't shine no shoes," Sim faintly said.

"Lay off him, Herman," Maybelle said.

Herman went on standing there. He said, "I'll thow it away for you, Uncle, if you don't want to read it."

Now Sim lifted his eyes, slowly bringing Herman into focus.

"Want me to thow it away for you?"

"Lay off him."

"It don't matter," Sim murmured. "Be awright."

"Okay, Uncle," Herman said and picked up the letter and flipped it into the trash box by the stove. "So long, Mr. Will." Then with a toss of his head he left the kitchen.

"Finish yo supper, Daddy."

Sim just managed to eat a little more. He would not think about it. He would not wonder what it said inside, in that shaky handwriting, and he would not let his mind drop back. If a dream tricked him in the night he would wake up and think about the next day and Hershel Rawls being in touch with him. But he had to walk a long time in the streets before he was tired enough to go to bed.

The next day was Friday but Sim did not go to work, he waited. He waited on the front porch, in the swing, watching every car approach and keep on past his house. The mailman did not even stop at his box and all day long the telephone was silent. At nearly four o'clock he set out walking. He walked to the Association office and after a little pause outside went straight in, straight up to the desk and the woman who had skin like a white woman. She gave him the smile that somehow had been more comfort to him yesterday and said Yes, Mr. Rawls would have it by now, because she had put it in the safe last night. That was not what she had said she would do. "How he gon know who hit come from?" Sim said. That smile again. Because she had written it on the envelope, in big letters: Mr. Sam Denny. "Hit's Sim," Sim said. "*Sim* Denny." She was sorry, she would fix that. And Mr. Rawls would be in touch with him. Behind her that door with the pane of glass you could not see through looked as if it might have been nailed shut.

It did not happen the next day either but the day after that would be Sunday. By Saturday night he had got it in his head that Sunday would be the day. It would be at church, maybe, and people would know and maybe, just maybe, when the time came for announcements Brother Dick would speak it out from the pulpit. Then Sunday and meeting in the morning and evening both went by and it did not happen. He went back to work on Monday.

Something did happen on Monday night but it was not at all what Sim was waiting for. It was in the newspaper that Maybelle showed him. "Yo white folks done died, Daddy." He stared at it for a couple of minutes at least, though he never got past understanding that it had happened last night at the hospital. At the hospital. It was like his mind had got stuck on this fact—this and the thought that he never had been to a hospital and never would go to one. He kept thinking this, just this one thing, on until he finally went to sleep that night.

Such as it was, what Sim had been waiting for came to him on Wednesday, after a long day in which he had put on a cement floor a surface like a pool of water that mirrored a clouded sky. It was a letter and Hershel Rawls' name was signed. ". . . your generous gift . . . men like you . . ." it said. He showed it to Maybelle, who only shook her head and gave a sigh. He did not show it or even mention it to Herman. He put it in his pocket. When he got to his room after supper he read the letter again and put it in his cabinet drawer. Then, conscious how his body ached, he lay down on his bed without undressing and went to sleep.

The next afternoon while Sim was down on his knees drawing his float with long sweeping strokes across the wet cement his breath stopped on him. He had to fight to get it back. It came with pain and then he lost it again. This kept on until Tod Nells, alarmed, led him off to the car and drove him home. Sim was better by then. He made Tod go away and went around the house to his room and got on his bed.

Maybelle appeared half an hour later (Tod had found her at a neighbor's down the street) and wanted Sim to go to the hospital. He said he wasn't going to no hospital, that he was all right now, but Maybelle called them anyway. They came and took him, over his protests, by force really, and carried him on a stretcher into an elevator and up and into one of those windowless dim-yellow hospital rooms.

Sim died on the night of the next day. They had thought he was much better, out of the woods now, and just an hour before he died said it would be all right for him to have a visitor or two, if he wanted. A little later Brother Dick appeared and the nurse went into Sim's room ahead of him. Sim was lying on his back with his face turned the other way, toward the wall. He seemed not to hear the nurse the first time she spoke to him. "Mr. Denny, it's Brother Dick," she repeated. "He's come to visit you."

Still there was silence for a few more seconds.

"Mr. Denny." The nurse could see that his eyes were open.

"Tell him go way." Nothing but his lips moved.

The nurse was surprised and made another brief try. She got the same answer, spoken exactly as before, and she had to go out and send Brother Dick away with a little bit of a lie.

Half an hour later the nurse was in Sim's room again, to check on him. He was still lying with his face to the wall. She heard him say faintly again, "Tell him go way."

"He left a long time ago, Mr. Denny."

"He out there. Got a letter fo me. Don't want to see no white folks." There was a pause. "Don't want to see no kind of folks."

He said nothing else, would not answer the nurse, and about twenty minutes later she found him dead.

NANCY FLETCHER-BLUME

Secrets of Southern Front Porches

Secrets. Dreams. Joys. Heartbreaks. Could a stranger passing by, quickly glancing, but know what drama, what memories, what portraits are painted on our simple front porches as families, close friends, and neighbors sit rocking, whiling away the lazy days and evenings of hot Southern summers.

In the diary of my life, more secrets have been divulged, more celebrations of great joy, and the too-often heart-wrenching of a grief shared on porches than any other place in our homes.

My earliest memories are of standing in the first breath of springtime, watching my mother as she carefully painted the wooden floor of our large sitting porch. Dipping the brush down into the paint can, methodically painting each board with long strokes of "Battleship Gray," she told me this was the color—when I had asked for red—that my daddy always painted the porch. Daddy was somewhere in the Pacific.

Pots of fiery-red geraniums soon filled this porch, along with snow-white painted rocking chairs with fluffy cotton cushions that my grandmother made. She kept a "RAGG" bag of scraps from alterations she did for several family members, and its contents would remind me of my never-ending supply of cousins, aunts, and sometimes even an uncle, as I recognized these scraps on the cushions. My grandmother gave no thought to matching. She just sewed. And so we sat and rocked on kaleidoscopes of color.

All through the long summer afternoons and evenings, the women on our street would gather, sitting and rocking on this colorful porch, drinking pitchers of ice tea filled with the petals of my grandmother's orange nasturtiums and sprigs of mint grown in the wet earth behind our wellhouse.

The children sat on the floor by my grandmother and our mothers. Their conversations were always about flowers, our school clothes, and recipes. But these conversations took on a different twist when children were not around. Sent inside to play with paper dolls so adults could talk, I would sometimes go out the back door and slip around to one of my favorite hiding places—behind the huge blue and purple hydrangea bushes alongside our porch—where I would secretly listen. They spoke in low voices of rationing stamps, censored mail, war bonds, someone's brother, son, or husband being brought back from "somewhere" in Italy, and of a new star hanging in the window of another neighbor's home.

Once—it was a July day filled with humid, heavy afternoon showers—we sat on the porch with several neighbors, and a lady who had not visited before ran up the paved walk. Grandmother had called out to her, asking her to sit awhile until the rain was over. She sat down on the gray, wooden floor beside me, declining the offer of a chair. I watched as she smoothed her thin, wet, purple skirt, while drops of water trickled slowly down her legs. She patted my hand, smiling, and asked if I liked her purple "broomstick" skirt. I immediately wanted one just like it and to have her for a friend. My grandmother told me later on when I asked about the skirt that the word and custom were brought into our country by the slaves, as they would "jump the broom" to seal their vows because the laws of our land did not allow them to marry.

SECRETS OF SOUTHERN FRONT PORCHES

Several of the neighbors had brought letters from overseas to share, and after one or two were read, this new lady, shaking her skirt and getting up off the floor to leave, explained she was not much for letter-writing and guessed "he" would just have to wait for home news. As she walked away, I remember the quiet, except for the slow dripping of water running down the gutters.

One of the neighbor ladies broke the silence, saying that it was such a shame, him being away and all that, the uncles coming and going, sometimes leaving early in the mornings. I thought that so strange. Uncles? My uncle, being my mother's baby brother, came almost every Saturday morning around noon, fixed anything that needed fixing, and then sat at lunch with my mother, grandmother, and me. I never saw my new friend again. It was later said on our porch that she just up and moved away.

One by one, all the men on our street came home, and their voices would blend deep into the night as porches again filled on those hot summers. Conversations were different. I watched as my daddy would pull my mother's rocking chair closer, his hand reaching, touching her auburn hair. Then pulling me close, he would tell us he always somehow knew he'd come back home to his girls. He also told my mother and me, one late evening, that he'd never put his feet in ocean water again. He did not.

Conversations on our porch now were all about the GI Bill, which made it possible for my daddy to return to school, taking night classes while working in the daytime. He also told us that he now could get a VA loan, which was available for servicemen and women, and we could soon get a larger house.

We moved early the following year to a new subdivision. This house had a large porch, and it did not take long for my mother and daddy to create beauty there. The floors were painted Battleship Gray, and white banisters were filled with pots of blood-red geraniums, baby-pink petunias, and my grandmother's ever-blooming array of gypsy-colored cushions.

We made new friends and neighbors, as folks walking by were greeted and asked to come and "sit a spell." By the end of that summer, I knew almost everyone in the neighborhood and was now included in more of the adult conversations.

It was on this porch where I stood poised for my mother to take a Kodak picture of me wearing my first long gown. It was baby blue, for my music recital. My parents had sat on the porch listening as I sat at the living-room piano, practicing over and over "The Triumphal March" from *Aida*. My daddy told me that my hard work had paid off, as my teacher was so happy with the performance that she invited me to play for the ladies at one of the monthly DAR meetings.

Standing on the steps of this porch in a mid-April's drizzling rain, I received my first sweet kiss from an early teen crush. On the long summer nights that followed and on into the fall, I would sit at night with my girlfriends, whispering about first kisses, clothes, and the taste of our Tangee lipsticks. On this porch, we vowed to keep these secrets and hold our friendships forever. But these conversations took on a different twist when adults came out and joined us.

I also had my first heartbreak standing on the steps of this porch. The mother of one of my best friends sat several afternoons, rocking and speaking quietly with my mother. I found them wiping away tears, and when I asked about my friend, I was told that she had gone away to live with her aunt for a while. She had left and not told me goodbye.

A few years later, on an early June's night, the boy I would eventually marry sat beside me in our porch rockers and told of his love for me. It was on this porch, beside a pot filled with red geraniums, that I left a note for my mother and daddy. I crossed the state line into Georgia and married my young love. It was on a Sunday night, while others were in church. I was fourteen years old.

For the first time in my life I had to find my own place of comfort on a different porch. This porch, deep in the dense kudzu gullies of South Carolina up-country, was filled with painted dark-green rockers, lush flowering plants, and heavy hanging purple wisteria vines that flowed up and over the roof of this rambling white farmhouse. Porch conversations here were different and foreign to me. They were about crops, weather, seining for fish, and exciting tales of the hunt. Some evening conversations were simply speculative, being about the comings and goings of cars and trucks that could be seen and heard going up the drives of neighboring farms.

There is something magical in going back home to your old porch, the porch of your parents, one that has heard and kept a young girl's secrets. On a late summer's evening, Grandmother and I sat rocking, breathing the heavy sweet scent of August lilies, talking of her "ragg-muffin" cotton cushions and "Now, in my day . . . ." I took her hand, telling her my new secret of the tiny life I carried. It was a first for this porch.

On a cold and bitter March day, my parents' gray porch stood stark and empty of all its woven magic of rockers and colorful flowers. I hugged the last of my cousins, aunts, and uncles as they left for their homes after we had shed our tears, shared our stories, and divided the "RAGG" cushions. We had said goodbye to Grandmother. My first son was born ten days later.

Over the years, our little family grew to three children, all boys. Our lives changed, but the porches did not. I was always drawn down to the wisteria-covered porch and the love of my husband's large family. Many late Sunday afternoons, my husband and I would sit with his parents, brothers, and their spouses, talking of the unrest and times.

It was the Sixties, and it seemed to me that the whole world was shifting, quickly, a world for which I was not ready. I was privy to hearing sad and terrible things on this porch, as conversations took on much deeper, painful, and many-layered twists.

Our innocent children played outside, running free in the heat of late summer afternoons, while we sat fanning, listening, drinking ice tea on this flowered, vine-covered porch. The males of the family were speaking in low voices, repeating stories they had heard of Night Riders, the Klan, bloody beatings, students watered down with hoses and shot. These porch conversations of Montgomery and Selma, now part of history, will forever remain with me.

On one Sunday afternoon, the shaded porch was crowded with family. Most of the conversation that day never strayed far from the horror of more killings in the small low-country town of Orangeburg, South Carolina. The newspapers carried this story and told of students being shot in the soles of their feet as they lay dead in the street. This would later come to be known as the Orangeburg Massacre.

I felt fear on this porch for the first time, as we had both FBI and state troopers in our family, all living in low-country South Carolina towns. My mother-in-law and I went to the family church on a Wednesday night, where she said a prayer for her sons that they would not be called in to go to these places, not be a part of this terrible racial violence. I realized more and more that my safe world of the porch had expanded and gone somewhere I did not want to go.

Late one August evening, a male member of the family found me sitting alone rocking. He told me he was leaving to live in another place several states away. He knew other family members would not understand. He told me he had to be true to himself and had to live his life in a different way—a way that could never be discussed by family, in polite conversation. At that time I was innocent of his reasons, but I knew his confiding in me should be a secret, well guarded.

A few years later, my husband, three sons, and I moved to Tennessee for a job. The new house had a very small front stoop, so we usually retreated to a large back patio for our deep conversations. Sometimes I would try to capture the feel of "porch" as I planted red geraniums in pots, and occasionally sat on the steps of the small stoop. We made new friends, and when they came, we stood in the yard talking or invited them to the back patio, or inside. It just wasn't the same.

The last week of May that year was sunny and bright. Saturday morning I sat on the stoop for a few minutes, missing my porch in South Carolina and all its flowers, but then left to do errands, leaving my family behind for fun things they had planned.

When I returned, driving down my street and turning into my driveway, I saw two of my friends standing on my small front stoop. I got out of my car and walked to them. They spoke, and my world was changed forever. We lost our youngest son that morning. He was eight years old. I have very deep, gray memories of me sitting on the steps of that stoop, rocking back and forth for a long time until they told me it was time to go inside.

Three days later we returned to the family cemetery, and the South Carolina home and porch of my childhood. Sitting in rockers on the familiar, brightly colored porch, were my mother, daddy, and the dark, row-braided woman who had helped raise my children. She had rocked our babies on this porch. She got to me first.

Many years and many porches later, after the recent heartbreaking loss of my beloved middle son, I sit on a porch here in Tennessee, on this day, his fiftieth birthday. It is a peaceful porch, filled with beautiful brown wicker, wonderfully fat cushions, ceiling fans, and dark jungle-green potted plants and trees. It is a porch where music filters softly through hidden speakers, along with the sound of water flowing over rocks. But I am not alone on this day in late April. I am with my eldest son. And we both remember, without saying.

Our deepest conversation is unspoken. This day should have held laughter, cake, and candles. Instead we sit sipping on Scotch, listening to all of my son's favorite songs, and talk of past porches, long-gone families, tales of the hunt, until way into the dark night.

I have traveled back several times to the old porches of my South Carolina homes. The deserted yards are now tangled and overgrown, the thick wisteria vines gnarled and black. Where tulips grew, there is only brown earth. The towering magnolia tree, which gave children places to climb and shaded the porch for lifetimes, still has hidden, deep and high in its branches, the carved initials of our family's young boys.

All of the voices have long since gone from these porches, and they will forever hold their silence and secrets.

BILL PEACH

The Willing and the Unwilling

We watched for the mail carrier's car every day for a letter from Uncle Allen who was serving across Western Europe in World War II. Mammy, my grandmother, agonized over the killing and the dying. Granddaddy worried more about the dying. He said the killing was just a part of war.

Two young soldiers that we all knew were killed early in the war. A cousin was hit by a piece of shrapnel and was left with limited use of an arm. Young men who were not called for the draft felt the unspoken envy of military families, and volunteered for the Army or Navy. There was no refuge from the war.

I understood the deep anger of World War II veterans as they watched my generation burn flags, shout obscenities, march and carry signs, and question the moral integrity of our President and our secretaries of state and defense. The greatest generation watched the news at six and ten and tried to make sense of My Lai and Kent State while their sons and younger brothers were being shipped home in body bags.

For me, joining the Army Reserve was a moral compromise between being a draft-dodger and a draft-evader. After active duty or a weekend Reserve meeting, I couldn't wait to get out of my olive-drab fatigues and back into a civilian coat and tie.

I wondered if the older people were looking at my uniform and remembering a husband or son killed in France or the Pacific. How could I have told them that this war was a mistake and I was not brave and was not going to die defending freedom, or America, or God, or whatever their husbands and sons had died for? My conversations and confrontations with college and high school students left mixed impressions of my being either an unpatriotic, anti-war, draft-dodging hippie, or someone who burned huts and killed babies in Vietnam.

The horrible conduct of the American people during and following Vietnam was shameful on both sides. We treated the returning soldiers and campus protesters with hostility and open displays of contempt. I was part of the anger and also a target of that anger. I am proud to have worn a uniform that I had never wanted to put on for six years. I pledge allegiance to my country and my flag with the heart and soul of a veteran and an aging flower-child. I am honored to stand when veterans are being recognized, but feel unworthy to share applause with combat heroes.

I voted against Richard Nixon, and found comfort in his resignation. I questioned the logic and conduct of a war, and did so because I loved my country and my brothers-in-arms.

A relevant question arose recently when one congregation of the United Methodist Church offered sanctuary to military resistors who refused deployment to Iraq. Members of the media were quick to remind us that these men and women took an oath to serve and did so willingly. Does it make a difference when the military is all-volunteer rather than conscripted? Do the same rules apply to the willing and the unwilling? Can a young soldier or marine ever say, "This war is a mistake and I am not brave and I am not going to die in Iraq for freedom, or America, or God, or whatever they are dying for"?

THE WILLING AND THE UNWILLING

Our letters from Uncle Allen continued until the end of the war in Europe. He came home to loving parents and family and an admiring nation. He was greeted with parades and hugs and kisses, and never questioned the rightness of the war nor doubted the necessity of his service.

I often attribute to Mammy my reason for being a Liberal. She loved her God and her country and her only son, and dutifully accepted the thought of his dying. She just never spoke any good feelings about the war or the killing.

LAURIE MICHAUD-KAY

Raising Eyebrows

The article in the fashion section of our metropolitan newspaper raised my eyebrows. A primary requirement for the fall "look" was, indeed, a well-defined eyebrow. Arched, with hairs spiked upward, it would glamorize the eye and balance the other makeup "must dos" for the fashion season.

This presented a problem for me. Having spent my formative years in the Fifties and Sixties, I was familiar with the well-defined eyebrow. All the role models on TV had plucked and penciled brows that were artistically maneuvered to convey surprise, skepticism, or astonishment. Think Lucille Ball and Donna Reed. They never made an entrance without first facing the tweezers and a sharpened eyebrow pencil.

This standard of beauty was emulated in my home where my two older sisters tweezed and penciled eyebrows of distinction. Being an idolizing baby sister, I couldn't wait to be allowed to do the same. Especially since my eyebrows resembled two caterpillars at war over my nose. In a photograph of me at age thirteen, not even my snazzy aqua pleated skirt and matching V-neck sweater could compensate for the hairy line of brow that cut across my face.

So when permission was granted to pluck away, I did—under the brow for that sophisticated arch, and between the brows to show I really did have two eyebrows, not one. I especially kept after those pesky thick hairs that seemed to want to revive the caterpillar war. I tweezed and tweezed, and as with most things I do, I got carried away. My early years of determined eyebrow care resulted in arches that vanished just after they peaked and a broad open field where the caterpillars used to face off. And since I never got the hang of penciling in realistic-looking eyebrows (it looked like I'd used my niece's brown Crayola), I decided to embrace the new counterculture look. I abandoned my bra and hid my eyebrows under long hair and in-the-eyes bangs.

But as fashion morphed in the succeeding decades, so did I. Today, my bra's firmly in place and my hair is decidedly shorter—thus my dilemma with the emphasis on eyebrows.

Sighing as I look in the mirror, I study my brows. They still bear the stamp of my youthful exuberance—overplucked and undersized—and are now also faded with gray. To make matters worse, my genetic makeup has started contributing random dark hairs that grow to alarming lengths, sticking up at odd angles across the brow. I reach for my trusty tweezers, but my hand pauses.

To be *tres chic* this fall, I will *need* eyebrows. An eyebrow pencil is out. My niece gave up Crayolas twenty-some years ago, and my drawing skills have not improved. So, grasping at hairs, I make a mental list of possible remedies.

Tattoos. A tattoo artist could fill in the blanks on my brows. *Voilà!* Permanent brows of distinction. Wait a minute. Do those dots spell "MOTHER" when I turn my head to the left?

Mousse. Mousse makes hair look fuller. It can also achieve that spiky look, since mousse stiffens hair to industrial strength. I'd just have to stay out of rainy weather. A meltdown could leave saggy brows, with long hairs that I'd have to keep pushing out of my eyes all day.

Combing over. Taking a trick from hair-challenged men, I could allow my genetically produced eyebrow hairs to grow even longer and then carefully comb them over the arch of each brow and down the side to cover the bald spot. Windy days could be a problem, however. Nothing worse than having your eyebrows blowing in the breeze at a football game.

Brow toupees. With a little makeup glue and some false eyebrows (courtesy of our local theatrical group), I could amass a dazzling array of brows to choose from. I might even be able to match my hair color, something I haven't been able to do since high school.

Hair plugs. After all the pain of plucking, do I really want to establish *new* hair follicles, even if they grow (to paraphrase a popular TV commercial) real hair that I could swim with and get trimmed by a barber?

I sigh more loudly this time. So much for *tres chic*. Guess it's time to again let my bangs hang out.

Far out, man.

CHANCE CHAMBERS

Water from Heaven

Quy Nhon
March 14

Dear Adèle,

I don't expect this letter to find you since we haven't spoken in years and I'm certain you've moved. I know this because my aunt and uncle mailed you a Christmas card a few years ago and it came back. I'm sending it to the address I had for your cousin Philippe in Ugine, but I wouldn't be surprised if he's moved, too.

Mailing it from Vietnam probably won't help, either. I've been here traveling up-country in a bus for almost a week. The next couple of nights I'm staying at a hotel on the beach in Quy Nhon. The sun's starting to go down, but there's still enough light to write this letter out on the balcony.

Yesterday, I saw the place Dad died back in '67. The Ho Bo Woods mentioned on all the Army paperwork is gone now. There's a dusty village where ex-Viet Cong live across the road from South Vietnamese families. No ghosts there. Just people living their lives, curiously watching and graciously meeting the white tourists coming down their road in a bus.

Being here reminded me of that time you denied that France was ever at war with Vietnam. I was just out of college and beginning to learn about France's history here. I asked you about it and you declared that "No, France was never in Vietnam." I'll always wonder if you actually didn't know your own country colonized Indochina in the 19th century and fought a war here in the 1950s, or if you just didn't want to admit it. Well, I have photographs now to prove it. Monuments to battles with the French, old French forts, things like that.

Something else I still wonder is what Dad said to you. You know, that time you dreamed you saw his face and he spoke to you. You never would tell me for some reason.

Vietnam made me think of you, but there's another reason I'm writing. Mom died of lung cancer in December. Though we lost touch, I think you would want to know. Things got weird in the end, but you two became quite close those summers you visited. For a while there, I'm sure she thought you were a daughter-in-law in progress. I guess I did, too.

Are you someone's daughter-in-law now? I have a feeling you're not single. I had that same feeling those summers you stayed with us. It only mattered to me sometimes. Never on those afternoons with you in the guestroom. Nothing else mattered to me then except the way you looked up at me, your brown ringlets against the pillow, trying not to squint from the sun that shone through the blinds making shadow bars on your alpine skin.

Mom knew about us before we ever told her. She had a way of knowing things. She knew something had happened to Dad before my aunt looked out her bedroom window to see the man in the Army uniform walking up to the front porch of the house where they lived with my grandparents. Days earlier, she had felt sudden sharp pains in the same places Dad had been hit with shrapnel.

I don't sense things. I had no idea Mom was so sick until she was diagnosed very late. Sometimes I think if I were more tuned in, like she was, the fact she's gone would seem more real. Hell, it didn't even seem real when we spent all that time in the hospital, wearing masks like the commuters in Saigon.

That was the first time Mom had been hospitalized since I was born. She spent a lot of time in the hospital with me when I was young. I had pneumonia yearly. Did I ever tell you that? Green is infection; red is cause for more concern. Mom taught me to check the color of the congestion I coughed up. That and the oxygen tents are what I remember most about those days.

Then, one year I stopped having pneumonia. My last time in the hospital, my last year of elementary school, I decided I was done with it. The next year, it was like I reached out for life, tasting more, feeling more. That was the year I started writing you for that seventh-grade pen pal project.

I've been having more of these flashbacks since I became an orphan. Like on the plane between Taipei and Saigon, I remembered one day during the summer before I started high school. I was down the street from my house hanging with a guy named Phil who was a grade behind me. His sister, who was a year younger than Phil, was there, too. It started raining. So we ran to our houses, put on our bathing suits, came back and splashed around in this creek behind their house. There on the plane, I could feel the current rushing over my legs and drops breaking on my shoulders. I was there again; it was like a waking dream.

Mom shows up in my sleeping dreams now. She keeps coming around even though everybody in the dream knows she's gone.

A couple of weeks ago, I finally told her she had died and needed to go on to the other side. Suddenly, it was the next scene, dreams being poorly edited as they are, and she was telling me through a radio that she would see me one more time and then be gone forever. She had been on the other side and was coming back once more. I asked her if she had seen Dad. She said no, but she had found out that people lived on islands on the other side and, for some reason, he had to live on a separate island from her. The next scene was our last time together.

It was in a restaurant with round tables and maroon walls. She was meeting someone else there, too—a man—to take care of some sort of business. Something about her pending departure, I assume. She never said.

That's all there was before I woke up sweating saki and beer.

I had spent most of the night before at a sushi bar in my neighborhood. The owner, Ken, is from Japan; the rest of the staff is from Thailand and Laos. One of the sushi chefs, Jay from Thailand, used to drink with me until his wife—who works there as a waitress—got pregnant. Now they're both on the wagon. I like when Jay does shots because he screws up his face like he just drank a cup of hot cough medicine. Then he runs over to the sink behind the sushi bar and scoops a handful of water into his mouth while he's still making that face. It makes me laugh.

Jay's wife is pretty, with a smile that always seems on the verge of mischief. Sometimes they tease each other across the room. I can't understand what they're saying, but I can tell by their faces. Jay smiles shyly when his wife looks at him with a slightly wild look in her eyes.

One time Jay told me that his grandmother visited him after she died. He was awake when he saw her. It took a while for him to recognize her. When he did, he was a little afraid. Then she touched his forehead and he fell asleep.

The night I had the dream about Mom, I was pretty gone. So much so, I decided at one point earlier in the evening I wanted to tell a waitress, who goes by Sonny, that she was pretty in Lao. She had waited on me before and had told me her real name—which the saki kept me from remembering—means "water from heaven." I was used to seeing Sonny in her black waitress clothes, but that night she was wearing a yellow summer dress because she was off duty and having dinner with friends. Another sushi chef, who's also from Laos, told me what to say. He could have set me up in a big way. I knew he hadn't when I clumsily repeated the words and Sonny became very humble, smiled, and thanked me. But it didn't take long for her to mention that she was married. She knows the sway saki has over good sense, and was forgiving.

I ended up drinking so much that night that Jay drove me home. Just in time, as it turns out, because less than five minutes after he dropped me off, I was in the bathroom throwing up. After I threw up the second time, I noticed a small sliver of red on the side of the toilet bowl. I tried not to think about it and flushed, hoping the cascading water would wash it away so it would be gone in the morning. Then I collapsed sideways onto the bed and slipped into my dreamscape with Mom.

I haven't been drinking as much here in Vietnam. There's plenty of opportunity, between the toast-ready locals in cafes and bars and all the snake wine. But I keep getting distracted. Like right now, it's an effort to stay focused on this letter. It's getting dark and there must be at least thirty fishing boats off the shore with their lights on now. It looks like a floating city.

They've been gathering since this afternoon, when I walked down to the beach and sat there letting the South China Sea wash up on my feet and legs. I watched the fishermen cast their traps for a while, then wrote "Dad" and drew a peace sign in the sand. Less than thirty seconds later, a wave pushed the tide higher and erased them both.

I stayed there for a while, trying to convince myself that there really was something on the other side of all that water. I finally gave up and walked back to the hotel, stopping at the steps to wash the sand off my feet with water drawn from a bucket with a gourd.

You should see this place. Granite shower and sink. Bed turned down with flowers on the pillow every time you leave the room. The manager at the hotel is French, by the way. He brought my bags up to my room. I tried to tip him but he refused. That's how I learned he was the manager. He said it wouldn't be appropriate.

I'll end this. It's nearly too dark to see what I'm writing, and the fishing boats have most of my attention now. You'll probably never see this letter, but I'll still mail it somewhere between here and Dien Bien Phu. That's where our road trip ends before we fly back to Saigon. It's a place you might want to look up.

I would say I hope you're happy and not alone, but it doesn't matter to me. I'm only really moved by our past. Oh, and if you do get this, I would still like to know what Dad told you.

Tam biêt
Chance

NANCY FLETCHER-BLUME

Finger Diamonds

I have never cared for diamonds. Never owned one. As a voyeur I study them from afar as they grace other hands, sparking my mind to wander and explore each diamond's origin. I feel the sweltering days, dripping in the heat of the Congo. I see ebony men with colorful turbans, heaving and pulling at steel-wheeled carts on tracks, as they hotly breathe and work around King Solomon's mines. In the shade of the diamond-mineshaft's overhang, there is always a tearoom, with men of British dress sporting eye monocles, seated at tables. Crisp, white-jacketed waiters hover in the background, holding aloft trays of cane sugar and icy bowls of tart, yellow lemon slices.

I prefer a ring of plain gold or earthy jade. I hold my own gold ring, rubbing it into the palm of my hand, and I am in Zimbabwe, where monsoons bring torrential rains, sending mineworkers and families to high ground and the safety of their *rondavels,* built on stilts, with thatched and wooden roofs providing little shelter from the downpour. I close my eyes and hear the swirling tongues of many languages. Zulu-speaking natives raise their voices to carry over the din of English men yelling out commands as the natives labor hour after hour after hour.

Another turn of my ring and I travel to another time and place far away, where placer gold is washed from alluvial sands and gravels in shallow pans. I am in the southernmost Ural Mountains. I watch men with stout Mongol features, their eyes gleaming with thoughts of these golden flecks that flirt with them, tempting them to pan again another day.

And jade . . . I am off to Burma. The stone in this ring I now caress holds a blood drop. I can faintly see it through its emerald-green translucence. It is said that the old carvers would study in their hands, over months and months, a single piece of jade, visualizing its final shape, humbly permitting the stone to reveal its destined form. Did this blood drop speak? Did it say: I am encased? I am encased beneath a polished dome—but I am forever free.

I sit most hot summer nights, absent of rings on my hands, well into the evening on my porch, occasionally rocking, looking at stars and thinking of diamonds. They are everywhere.

Tonight I feel a stirring desire for finger diamonds. I search my cupboard shelves and see an old Mason fruit jar. I smile. A few hole-punches later and I am eagerly slipping off my shoes to walk barefooted, deep into the dew-wet grass. I reach upward into the humid night for the diamonds. One by one I place them in my jar. And now, sitting on my steps, I gently take these delicate diamonds and place them on my fingers. I allow myself but a few fleeting moments' enjoyment before I remove my diamonds and watch them take to air. I cannot follow them. They are forever free. I can only imagine.

GINGER MANLEY

Two Weddings, Four Divorces, and One Marriage

When I look at the fading photograph of my first wedding, I can still hear the rustle of crepe paper and feel its sharp edges against my five-year-old legs. I am standing in front of our fireplace in my childhood home, with my right arm crooked through the arm of the groom. He is dressed in a suit and tie, but he is missing some of his front teeth, a condition which is considered normal for some people in East Tennessee. In my family, though, it was a first for a bride to have a snaggle-toothed bridegroom, but, then, he was only seven.

On the groom's right, as maid of honor, is my best friend, five-year-old Sally, dressed in her own full-length crepe paper dress which was made for her, as was mine, by my mother. To my left is four-year-old Lynda, wearing a tutu version of the paper outfits. She is holding a small square white satin pillow on which is secured the wedding ring. She has never felt sweet waxy lipstick before, so her puckered-up mouth tells me that she is trying to absorb the sensation of this grown-up application, along with the scratching of the crepe paper. This was definitely a quickie wedding—we all had to be in bed by eight so we could go to school the next day. After we had paraded through the bridal shower, for which we were decked out, we discarded our wedding attire and dissolved our union.

My second divorce took place when I was in seventh grade, following a whirlwind romance in which I was kissed for the first time. I signed on for life with that smooch, but alas, he wanted to taste other girls, so six weeks after he gave me his metal dog tags as a token of his enduring love, he moved on to someone else and left me brokenhearted. His red hair and freckles burrowed themselves into my heart, and to this day, whenever a redheaded guy smiles at me, I melt a little.

Then in high school and in college I fell twice more—conflicted and tempestuous romances in which I thought I was the one and only, but they were operating off another script. Neither was man enough to tell me we were through. They just called me up when they needed something, like a female's body, and I was there to help them out. It's tough to be a divorcee when you don't know the divorce has even happened. So I tied three knots around my heart and vowed never to let anyone in again. That is not to say I wrote men off. Not true. I just vowed not to let them get to me again. And it worked for years.

In the meantime I had another quickie wedding, this time the more traditional kind, where the bride is pregnant and the groom is sweating bullets. Well, maybe dodging bullets. Since I had only met the groom two months before our little trip down the aisle, I can see why everyone in attendance hesitated to buy good china as a wedding present when paper plates were probably more appropriate. But lust is a funny thing, and falling in lust is a lot more exciting than falling in mere love. Of course, lust burns itself out faster, too, but by then, if a baby is on the way, what choices does one have?

Sometimes it didn't seem like there were very many choices. By the time we were at our five-year anniversary, we had two children and had hit bottom financially. We talked about divorcing and concluded that we were too poor to be able to afford

TWO WEDDINGS, FOUR DIVORCES, AND ONE MARRIAGE

that solution, so we plowed on. At the ten-year mark, things were temporarily looking up, with the finances a little improved and more education behind us as preparation for a future. At fifteen years, however, the rosy glow was completely gone, and now it was just a matter of time until both children were out of high school and I could be alone. My heart was hardened, and my plan was to file for divorce the month after the youngest child left for college.

Then something happened. On my fortieth birthday he gave me an awesome present—he quit taking me for granted, and in turn, I stopped blaming him for all my troubles. One of those knots loosened and it felt pretty good. Then on my fiftieth birthday, he tried to give me a gift he thought I would find hilarious. It wasn't, and as I stood on stage before one hundred of our friends, being roasted, when I had specifically asked for this not to happen, I chose to forgive this man with whom I had struggled in and out of lust and love for almost a quarter-century. By the next morning, the second knot was gone.

On my sixtieth birthday, we had a quiet dinner. Many losses had occurred in our lives over the past few years, and we were just grateful to be able to sit down across from each other and enjoy a meal together. We celebrated our thirty-eighth wedding anniversary in England in September of that year, on the date that his stepmother was memorialized in her home church, after she had died during our visit to her. Since I had been the last person to see her alive and she had died unexpectedly, there was a brief time when the coroner had pondered whether I might have had something to do with her death. Fortunately the inquest cleared me of any wrong-doing, but the thought of my being locked away in a British jail had literally gripped my husband's heart, sending him into a cascade of cardiac irregularities. At one point, before we knew the outcome of the coroner's inquest, he looked at me through dripping eyes and said, "I would be devastated if something happened to you."

That was the gift that untied the third knot. Choice after choice, day after day, our lives moved toward and away from each other for going-on-forty-one years, and the cord that bound my heart to keep out the pain now encircles him.

Two weddings.

Four divorces.

One marriage.

21

ANGELA BRITNELL

Tuesday Rendezvous

Ellie glanced anxiously at her watch and then out at the car park for about the twentieth time. He'd promised to be on time today. He knew she daren't be late getting home. It would lead to too many questions.

She studied her reflection in the window, wishing she'd made an effort and changed from her standard jeans and sweatshirt. Ellie hastily pulled out her lipstick, pale pink and worn down to a nub, and slicked some on. She hoped it cheered her tired complexion a little, but that was probably wishful thinking.

Rain drizzled down the coffee shop window, making it hard to see. She forced herself to look away, take a sip of her rapidly cooling latte, and pretend to read the celebrity gossip magazine she'd chosen off the display stand. What must it be like if your only problem was what designer dress to wear that night and which party to go to? She couldn't imagine and wasn't likely ever to find out.

"Hey, gorgeous." Jude stood in front of her, smiling directly into her heart. Tall, handsome, and hers alone for the next half-hour.

Ellie smiled back, longing to do so much more, but reminding herself where they were. She caught the pretty, young blond girl at the next table staring at Jude, but he didn't notice. When they first met she'd worried about falling in love with a man this handsome, but he was completely oblivious to the effect he had on women. Jude always told her she was the beautiful one and laughed out loud the day she compared him to a Michelangelo statue. It was the only time she'd seen him blush a heated bright red.

Jude hated what they were doing. He wasn't the sort of man to enjoy sneaking around, but if they wanted to be together, what choice did they have? It wasn't as if she relished it any more than he did. This wasn't supposed to have become a long-term thing. A couple of weeks, a few fun dates, and their lives would go back to normal. But it wasn't working out that way. There seemed no end in sight.

"What's your day been like?" His sharp green eyes focused steadily on her, making Ellie shiver. They always did. She wanted to tell him the truth, but didn't intend to waste the sliver of time they had by whining. Jude's large, capable, tanned hands with traces of oil still under the nails, held hers until the tension eating at her eased enough for her to speak. The man understood her so well, it made Ellie ache inside.

"Oh, the usual. Mother's saying she'll go home next week, but we've heard that before and . . ." Disbelief resonated in her voice, as much as she tried to sound positive.

Jude attempted a laugh, but the corners of his mouth never moved and his eyes didn't do that irresistible crease at the edges. For a second his glance dropped to the table and he fiddled with his coffee cup. A sigh broke loose as he lifted his head back up to meet her curiosity. "I got a good offer at work today." There was a touch of defiance in his voice, and he waited for her to ask for more details.

Ellie's throat tightened uncomfortably, keeping her silent. It didn't take a genius to see where this was going.

"Tom West wants me to head up the new team they're forming. It'd mean a lot more travel, going around to all the branches in the Southwest. I'd still be home every weekend, though, and the extra money would help."

Ellie's skin paled until she felt her freckles sticking out on stalks. Their time together was short enough now and this would make it worse.

His deep voice remained measured and calm. "We can't go on this way, love."

That wasn't telling her anything she didn't already know. Ellie sensed him covering the fact that he was torn up inside, but he was old school where the notion of a man showing emotion was concerned. It was something that made her love him more yet frustrated her at the same time.

"But the extra hours. I need you around more, not . . ." She was too afraid to finish the sentence.

"Think about it. It could help get us out of all . . . this . . . sooner." His hand stroked down the side of her face and lingered on her jaw.

The hurt in his eyes pained Ellie. He was right. They would have to make a decision soon. There weren't many options.

"I suppose we'd better get going, Ellie. Same time next Tuesday? You want to try the Bluebird Café for a change?"

She gave a slight nod, as tears filmed her vision. Jude took her hand and slowly led her outside. Normally when they came here, they stopped to browse through the new books, taking pleasure in deciding what they'd buy if money weren't so short, but neither could keep the pretence going today.

Ellie squeezed his hand tight, relishing the warmth of his skin against hers, tucking the memory away for the lonely hours. This was silly. Weren't they too old to feel this way about each other?

He'd parked his work van next to her little red Mini with no other cars nearby—islands marooned in a sea of deep puddles. It gave Ellie a burst of strength when she saw that, as if they stood together against anything the world could throw at them.

Jude placed his hands on her shoulders and leaned Ellie up against her wet car. He began kissing her like a teenager making the most of the last five minutes of his curfew. As she responded, it flashed through her mind what they must look like to anyone watching.

A man and a woman who'd arrived in two separate cars, been engaged in intense conversation oblivious to everything around them, and who were now wrapped around each other. It'd be so obvious what they were up to.

At their far-too-small home, a bad-tempered mother recovering from knee surgery had taken up what seemed to be permanent residence in their bedroom. There was also an out-of-work teenage son with too much time on his hands. Then their much loved, but unexpected, one-year-old twin daughters took up the only other bedroom. Ellie joined them there at night, sleeping on a single inflatable mattress that regularly deflated, leaving her with a sore back from the hard floor. Jude, constantly tired and frustrated, slept on a much-too-short sofa that drooped in the middle from years of hard use.

Something had to give—or it would be their marriage of over twenty years that collapsed, sagging under weighty responsibilities. They'd seen it happen to far too many of their friends.

Voilà—the Tuesday Rendezvous. Sneaking away to a different place each week—anywhere they could finish a sentence, hold hands, and reconnect. To remind themselves what it was all about.

Jude tipped her chin up to meet his fierce stare. "It'll be okay, Ellie. We'll laugh about this soon. Hey, we might even continue doing it when we don't have to." His voice dropped to a husky whisper. "Have you seen the looks that young girl inside by the window is giving us? She's convinced we're up to wicked things. At our age, I'd say that's a compliment."

"Well. Let's give her something to look at, then." Ellie cradled his loving face and gave him a big, deep kiss for the entire world to see.

CHRISTOPHER ALLEN

The Trauma, or Real Men Get Facials

Whatever else I am, I have come to the smarting realization that I am first and foremost a man. Take for instance my low threshold for pain (*sharp* to me is anything pointier than, say, a cantaloupe) or my undying love for anyone—anyone—who'll rub my back. As if these telltale signs weren't proof enough of my manhood, an experience I had while visiting my dear friend Lori in New York two years ago has made it painfully clear.

Yes, I'm writing about The Trauma, as I like to call it, from a literary distance of two years (of therapy). In fact, I'm just now *this* moment able to express what I've learned in those two years: 1) it's OK to cry; 2) the Koreans are not punishing us for The Conflict; and 3) one cannot drown in egg whites. To be honest, my therapist and I are still working on number three.

It was a sweaty August day in Manhattan. The city smelled like garbage stewing in soured milk, so Lori started going down her list of ways for us to pamper ourselves indoors.

"Let's get a facial."

"Let's sharpen knives on our eyeballs," I countered.

"Oh, come on. It's so . . . so . . ."

"Expensive? Pointless? Girly?"

"Men get facials all the time."

"*Gay* men."

"You *are* gay."

True. So, all out of arguments, I followed Lori out the door in search of someone to express our pores. After searching most of the morning in the blistering heat, Lori, who didn't even need a facial, chose a cosmetologist's salon because of the picture of Jesus in the window.

"We're Christians, too," Lori spouted as we entered the little shop. I suppose she thought we might get a discount.

"You porcelain doll!" the cosmetologist shrieked and started stroking Lori's face. Talk of perfect skin and God went on for quite a long time. I think I even read a couple of back issues of *Cosmopolitan* while I waited to be noticed.

Once we established the fact that I existed, and we explained to the little woman that I, although undeniably male, would also be having the thirty-minute deep-pore special, the woman led me down into what I now affectionately refer to as The Chamber, short for the egg-white-boarding chamber (sort of like water-boarding, but goopier).

All settled in the chair, which I'm sure had once been a dentist's chair, I smelled the pleasant aroma of eucalyptus-scented steam wafting toward my face. This might have been nice, but just before the steam reached my face, it took a turn and floated up to the ceiling.

"Dilate pore." My torturer-to-be smiled and left The Chamber to "mix egg white."

"Pore on ceiling maybe," I said in her accent and began to ask myself (in my own Southern drawl) if this facial hogwash was a good idea. "You're making a boil out of a blackhead." I chuckled to myself and leaned like a koala toward the eucalyptus steam.

For a deep-pore special that was supposed to last only thirty minutes, it was taking the woman a very long time to mix those egg whites. I wondered—as you might do at a busy brunch restaurant—if the eggs had hatched yet.

Then suddenly, delicate little hands came from nowhere and began massaging my face with a gritty paste. I must have fallen asleep.

"Mild exfoliating cleanser," the woman whispered. "Your girlfriend pretty," she said. "Porcelain doll."

Yeah, yeah, yeah. It's about *my* skin now, and I was just about to tell her this when the woman pinched the heart and soul out of a poor, helpless pore on the tip of my blameless nose. I just have to say that my nose has never done anything to anyone. It has a strict policy of keeping itself out of everyone else's business.

"Oooohhh! Yuck. Bad! Bad! Bad!" the woman bleated.

I wish I could have imagined her playfully squeezing sebum out of that pore like a Play-Doh log—something cute and humorous, though equally disgusting, to give us all a good tickle. But I was in shock, and my torturer had already proceeded to her next victim.

"Oh, my . . . !" I bit my tongue, not wanting to jeopardize our Christian discount. My body went rigid, much like a body might do if attacked by a bear or an evil spirit.

"You OK, you OK. You need two treatment," she said, and pinched again.

"Lord God!"

"Maybe three."

Then—I couldn't help it—a tear-shaped drop of fluid from the lachrymal gland in my left eye rolled down my cheek.

"Oh, you cry? You cry." She laughed. The woman actually guffawed. "You cry!"

So that we're all on the same page here, I did not cry. My lachrymal gland watered. You know, like when you cut onions, or get caustic chemicals in your eyes, or when you have open-heart surgery without anesthetic. My eye watered. Just the left one. I'm not in denial. I know now that it's OK to cry, but in this particular situation, my therapist and I have come to the conclusion that I did *not* cry.

"OK, OK, OK, Mister," she purred. "You calm down. Where you from? You like New York? Pretty day, huh? It hot, but pretty. Stink a little." She was making pleasant, whispery conversation, hoping, I guess, that I would stop convulsing. She might as well have been piercing my side repeatedly with a switchblade, while asking if I could recommend a good restaurant in the neighborhood. I couldn't remember where I was from. Had the day been hot but pretty? I answered all of her questions with a quivery "Uh-uh-huh." She handed me a tissue. I said, "Uh-uh-huh."

"Egg white soothe pain and stop bleeding. Like yin and yang," she said and began glopping goop all over my face. Then—as was her habit—she left the room, but not without a cute little Parthian shot: "Ahh, you have egg on face. Funny joke, huh?"

Yes, very funny, I thought, sitting there for the next fifteen minutes, a trembling meringue, wondering how big the difference was between what had come out of my pores and what was seeping in now. And can I just say that, not being a mouth-breather, having egg whites coagulating in one's nose is harrowing. I appreciate air so much more now.

When it was all over (is it ever really over?), I moped upstairs for my pedicure. As I passed dear Lori on her way to The Chamber, I guess I could have warned her, but honestly, knowing **Lori** as I do, I was sure that if the woman tried to hurt her, **Lori**, the porcelain doll, would break her arm.

"Your nose is kind of red," she said in passing.

"Uh-uh-huh."

My pedicurist, a sweet young thing, kept looking up **at me** and smiling. She probably didn't get many male **customers.**

I entertained the notion that she found me unusually handsome and bold for penetrating this female domain. Or rich husband material? Maybe she thought I was Brad Pitt or at least a Backstreet Boy. She was a Christian, so maybe, toweling off my feet, she was having a Mary Magdalene fantasy.

"Oh, uh . . . Honey?" I tittered. "That kind of tickles a bit."

"Sorry," she said and continued buffing the toenail on my little toe. "We wouldn't want you to . . . cry!" And then she giggled outright.

"Watered," I corrected, retracting my foot. "My left eye watered."

"Whatever. What polish you want?" She grabbed my foot back and nodded toward a wall of nail polish that remarkably resembled the gay rainbow flag.

Of course I related the traumatic events to Lori on the way home: the manly misery-needing-company sort of thing.

"Yeah. May told me you cried," she said, not exactly giving my misery the kind of company it needed.

"She told you her name?"

"We prayed for you."

"Well, that's nice . . . I guess."

May is probably "praying" for me with another client right now—sniggering something about a porcelain doll's friend who had enough goo in his pores to fill a goo bucket. So if you've prayed for my pores with a KoreAmerican Christian cosmetologist named May (we got the discount), please tell her that I didn't cry. My left eye watered. It's an involuntary process stimulated by the autonomic nervous system. And, just in case you also talked to that sassy pedicurist, I chose clear nail polish—not tulip primavera pink, no matter what she says.

23

CURRIE ALEXANDER POWERS

Losing Richard

I can't think of New Orleans without thinking about Richard. She fell in August of 2005. Richard was diagnosed in July of 2006. Both their lives hung in the balance for a year. New Orleans was just starting to heal two years later. Richard took the long walk June 15, 2007.

She held the music. Richard played it.

New Orleans may be the birthplace of jazz, with the trumpet standing as the elegant icon of the genre, but the piano players are her dark-horse children, full of boogie-woogie and devilment. Jelly Roll Morton, Roosevelt Sykes, Henry Roeland "Professor Longhair" Byrd, and James Booker—Richard's hero—created the gumbo that is New Orleans music—a masala of jazz, blues, gospel, and Cuban rhythms.

I knew Richard in many different cities, but the image of him in New Orleans is the one that lingers. He belonged there among the piano greats because he was one of them.

My first trip to New Orleans was in 1990 for Jazz Fest. It was like going home. Music leaked out of every crack. The smell of food, damp, garbage, sweat, and muddy water was flagrant and unabashed, refusing to be hidden. Coming from the bleached-clean streets of Toronto, I felt relief and comfort in a city that just let it all hang out. I came home with the sound of Snooks Eaglin and The Zion Harmonizers ringing in my ears, and knew I'd go back for more.

In August of '97 I found myself there again, this time with a band of eager musicians. Richard was among them. The rest of us were gawky foreigners, eyes skyward like dumbstruck tourists, but Richard glided out of the airport coolly, immediately at home. At the time, I thought it was his extra years of living, ten years older than the rest of us, and that he had played everywhere from Los Angeles to Montgomery, ridden the crest of success, and seen the underbelly of the music business. In hindsight, it was neither. Richard was just cool.

By the time I met Richard in 1989, he was already a part of musical history.

He came from the suburbs of Toronto, and in 1961, at the age of fifteen, began his music career as an organist. He didn't play in just any church. He played in *The* Church—Maple Leaf Gardens, home of the Toronto Maple Leafs. He couldn't have scored a more *Canadian* gig and remained a devoted hockey fan for the rest of his life. Yet, Richard was always more international in his attitude. At eighteen, he hit the road with Rompin' Ronnie Hawkins, lived on beer and fast food, and probably saw more whores and fringe dwellers than he should have. It was a hard initiation, but it toughened him for the next twenty years on the road. In 1969 he hit the big time when Janis Joplin plucked a handful of Canadian musicians to be her Full Tilt Boogie Band. He was twenty-three years old. But he had the hands, long popsicle-stick fingers like Fess, and a left hand that knew how to thunder the bass notes and leap tall octaves in a single bound. No one could stomp that left-hand rhythm like Richard. That is what set him apart from all the other piano players.

Richard never talked about playing with Janis Joplin, but it was a badge of honor we all respected. He was modest that way.

When we arrived in New Orleans that August to work at Kingsway Studio, Germaine Wells' old house at the corner of

Esplanade and Chartres, the temperature was 95 every day and the wall of humidity that hit you as you stepped outside was a force you could not fight. We succumbed willingly.

We spent a good deal of time talking about music, sitting around the kitchen table in between takes. There were always gems that slipped out of Richard in a nonchalant way. I had just discovered Professor Longhair and was goggle-eyed picturing him walking down the same streets I walked in the French Quarter. Richard piped up then and surprised the hell out of me. He said that when he lived in Woodstock, New York, Fess came up to record. Richard hung around with him at Bearsville Studio, studied his left hand, learned a few tricks on how to play barrelhouse. *He'd been in the same room with the master.* He traded jokes with the man who'd written "Tipatina" and "Mardi Gras in New Orleans." I spent the rest of the week looking sidelong at Richard, wondering what other things he'd never mentioned. Years later I learned that he went away one weekend for a "little gig" and forgot to mention to his family that it was for the Clinton inauguration.

All that Richard was came out in New Orleans. I have a clear picture of him sitting on the grand staircase at Kingsway, skinny legs bent, a pad of manuscript paper across his knees as he worked on horn charts for the session that weekend. In that moment he was Duke Ellington, mastering an arrangement. And when the horn players came in and laid down their parts in the front hall with its sky-high ceilings, the elegant weave of notes that Richard had written bloomed like a delicate flower. I still get goosebumps remembering that sound. I get choked up remembering Richard sitting there with a pile of horn charts on his knee, listening to the notes he'd heard in his head coming alive in the air, a look of wonder, gratification, and pride on his face.

Later that weekend, Richard was sitting at the grand piano in the living room, which was the recording floor as well as the control room. It was a beautiful old piano, and I remember thinking that Richard deserved to play an instrument of that quality all the time, and yet he didn't. Sometimes they were battle-scarred uprights, badly out of tune. Or cheap synthesizers on loan. He didn't care. A set of keys was a set of keys. It was what he could do with them that mattered. Richard never seemed to acknowledge how good he was. He wasn't a prima donna, when he had every right to be. He never complained about the accommodations or having to haul his own equipment. There was something fitting about seeing him sitting in a mansion in New Orleans amongst all that dark wood, the velvet curtains, antiques, and mosaic floors. He was deserving of such surroundings.

I can hear his laugh echoing in that big house, a soprano cackle that still had a lot of little boy in it. Richard was Peter Pan in many ways, single and childless, fond of silly pranks. But in New Orleans, he was a great musician amongst his peers, Dr. John and Allen Toussaint.

In August of 2005 I was sitting in a hotel room in Los Angeles. I was supposed to be writing the last few chapters of my novel. Instead I was glued to the TV watching an unstoppable black cloud roll toward New Orleans, then wipe her off the map. Almost two years later, another black cloud would roll in, and I would be standing at Richard's funeral with that same feeling of numbness and helplessness.

Since Hurricane Katrina I have vowed to help New Orleans rebuild. I donated my car, and every chance I get, go down there to support the tourist industry. I want her to return to her vibrancy. I want her to live again.

Richard is gone. I can't bring him back, but I can rebuild him every day, memory by memory. Musicians are fortunate to leave behind a legacy. Richard lives every time I put on a record of Janis Joplin, The Band, Colin Linden, or hear the theme from *Welcome Back, Kotter*.

New Orleans will get back her shine, but there will always be ghosts walking the streets and in the alleys. Ghosts of those who've gone before, Fess and Buddy Bolden, those who lived simple lives in the Lower 9th Ward and perished under the floodwaters. I will feel their presence each time I go there. And somewhere in that parade of spirits will be Richard's ghost, walking down Chartres Street or playing the piano in a cool dark room. He lives on in what we've lost. Every time I walk through the French Quarter, I will pay homage to him and what he gave, in a place where music is a million tiny droplets in the humid air, and where the soul-song of a city, tried and tested time and again, is like Richard. It can't be silenced.

Richard Bell
March 5, 1946 – June 15, 2007

CARROLL CHAMBERS MOTH

An Inquiry Regarding Louchelle Maxine Green

You ask me, "What do you remember about Louchelle Maxine Green?"

Louchelle came into my class late in the year, court ordered, I was told, which meant she was under eighteen. She preferred to be called Maxie.

Physically, she was tall for a girl, five-ten, maybe five-eleven, or maybe she just appeared tall. She was big, not seriously overweight, not what one would call buxom, more along the lines of *zaftig*. Big boned.

She had long brown hair, a bit straggly, which she wore down on occasion, but usually up, piled high on her head and steadied with a pencil, or in a bun, tied with a rubber band or a shoelace. And her eyes were blue, big blue eyes that hinted of mischief. She tried to act serious, when necessary, but her smile would crack just enough to let you know that school was a very small part of her life.

The reason Maxie was required to attend school was that she had been stopped by a cop. She was going a bit too fast and driving without a license. A valid license, apparently, was also a small part of her life. Upon further investigation by the authorities, there were reports of her writing checks with no money in her account. Maxie held to the belief that if she still had checks, there must be money in the bank. It appeared she had had many encounters with the police.

And so Maxie entered the world of academia and became part of my often-captive audience pursuing the hopefully serendipitous experience of visual art in my advanced class. She attended class most days, unless the weather was inclement, it was a half day, or she had yet another court appearance. Sometimes she slept and sometimes I let her sleep. Her projects were done quickly with the most minimal of lines and values—not sloppily, but with the necessity of someone who had more important things on her mind. She showed interest in one project, where her assigned objective was to design a childcare nursery for a hospital. While she was drawing the floor plan, she insisted on making it appear three-dimensional, which wouldn't translate on graph paper. This presented a problem with grading.

Her apparel was not unlike the other students': flannel shirts, probably her father's, jeans, and off-white sneakers—very large, heavy sneakers. Unlike the other girls in the class, she didn't have her nails done at thirty-five dollars a pop, nor did she have her hair cut at the beauty shop. While the girls discussed herbal shampoos, Maxie announced she washed her hair with a bar of brown Boraxo soap—harsh and abrasive, marketed for men like mechanics who get their hands dirty. This could explain the highlights in her hair, which changed if she stood too long in the sun. She considered cutting her hair once, but we talked her out of that because her hair framed those lovely eyes. Also, unlike the other girls, she never cut class for a hair appointment, but she did cut for one of her three jobs. Maxie cleaned houses and worked part-time hours at the Dixie Diner and the Flying F. Her duties were waiting tables and standing in for the short-order cook. She liked waiting tables because she made good tip money and she could always grab a meal at work. The downside was that she had to close on Thursdays and Sundays. Often she brought in leftovers in doggie bags from her job—brownies, stale doughnuts, cold pizza.

I was told that when Maxie was five, her mother had killed herself. I didn't ask why, and I'm not sure the other kids were even aware of it, as Maxie had moved away immediately afterward. Many remembered Maxie from kindergarten. We lived in a small town, and like all small towns, people knew most people's business: who went to church, and which church, and who didn't; who drank and who was sober; who slept with whom; and who not to take your car to for repairs. This community was so close, it was necessary to keep charts of family marriages so one didn't end up dating a first cousin (unless one wanted to—and judging from the population, evidently a few did).

After her mother's death, Maxie's daddy had moved around the country, mostly in the South, so besides her travel experiences, Maxie developed an unusual variation on a drawl that fascinated the other students. When she and her daddy returned to our town, I met her. She had few years in school. Few entries were noted in the system, but she was street smart. Her daddy evidently had exposed her to areas of experience outside the realm of small-town life.

Despite her lack of schooling, she was confident, hard-working, and creative. She was also personable, and I would even say generous. She resented school because school cut into her "work" time, and she had bills to pay.

She shared with me that her daddy had trouble holding a job. He had a disability, and she was basically responsible for her family, which consisted of the two of them. And Daddy had a girlfriend named Charlene. Maxie said Charlene was okay, but she'd been around the block more times than the ice-cream man.

At one time, Maxie had bought a house and owned a car, she told me, but she said she lost the house after a bad relationship. Her girlfriend she was dating "screwed" her, she said—took all the money out of the checking account and ran off. Maxie was now dating a girl in school, much to the dismay of the other students. "Every pot has a cover," she said. Skanks, the other kids called them.

Small-town life was hard put to embrace so radical a lifestyle, but she pushed on doing what was necessary to survive emotionally, financially, and in class. As to other people's opinions, she'd say, "I don't flippin' care," but I suspect she did. She told me once that she eventually wanted to become a nurse. My initial warning to myself was, "Never get sick."

I haven't seen Maxie in years, but I often think of her and remember a young girl who had a rough start and too much responsibility. I still pray she will make it.

So, to answer your question—"What do you remember about Louchelle Maxine Green?"—I remember her smile, her generosity, her "stick to it" attitude, her confidence, her toughness hiding a good and kind heart, but I have to smile when I think of a talent she had that gave us all a chuckle. Maxie gave the best imitation of a police siren that I have ever heard.

(25)

JAMES E. ROBINSON

Faith

My little sister has died.

Her name was—is—Mary Jennifer Robinson Turner. She died in the same way our mother died, of a drug overdose, and at nearly the same age. All of us who loved and truly knew her had been expecting it, in a way, for many years. That's the way of things, when the person you love is an addict. You pray for them and sometimes try to convince them to get help, but mostly all that does is make you feel just as crazy as they are. So you keep praying, asking and hoping for a miracle, because you know that even though the situation seems hopeless, well, you've seen miracles happen before, maybe even to you, in your own life.

We have to keep the faith, after all.

Because if God has created miracles in our own lives, miracles far beyond what we deserve, surely He will reach down and save someone else, someone far more pure and decent and childlike in her heart than we ever were or ever will be.

When Jennifer and I were little kids, we did what brothers and sisters do. We played together, fought, made up, and played together again as if we'd never been angry. Jennifer was the baby, three years younger. We clung to one another when bad things sometimes happened in our house. Whenever things began to feel dangerous, we'd hide together. And when things were quiet, we played a lot of make-believe. I guess all of us played a lot of make-believe back then. Back when there was a lot more fear than faith.

When she was very young, Jennifer was sweet and round-faced and beautiful. She had blonde hair and eyes the color of a perfect sky. I would sometimes tease her about her chubby cheeks, and one time I got mad at her and called her "hippo girl." She adored me, I know now, and when I called her this name, her face grew white with shame. I would give anything—anything at all—if I could go back to that place in time and take back those words. I wouldn't call her "hippo girl."

I would tell her she was as beautiful as any princess in any fairy tale. I would tell her that when she smiled, something like soft innocence would fall all around everyone in the room like spring rain. I would tell her not to be afraid, that this time I would do a better job of protecting her, somehow. I would look into those amazing azure eyes and tell her that sweet spirits like hers should never have to see violence or endure betrayal, and I would pray with her this time, like I could not then that she would choose all the things in life ahead that were as beautiful and graceful as she.

Being the youngest, Jennifer was the last child to graduate high school and leave home. She not only had to experience the worst times of dysfunction in our house, but she had to do so more or less alone. Our older sister Joette had married. I had run as far away as possible, into my own selfishness, my own fear and shame. I can't remember having ever given a single thought to what might happen to my little sister, my sick mother, or to anyone else in my family, for that matter. I only cared about myself.

Jennifer was the most tender-hearted child in the family by nature, and took more of the brunt of our mother's emotional illness related to bipolar disorder and addiction.

"What's wrong with Momma?" she asked one day, as if she had just been made aware of some long-hidden secret. She had ducked into my room for sanctuary. And perhaps it was at times like this when I loved my little sister the most—and yet felt most helpless.

"Nothing," I muttered, or something equally evasive. I just went on pretending, fantasizing... *Nothing's happening, nothing's wrong, just leave it alone.*

As a family we had stopped talking much by then. How desperately we needed each other, and how hard we tried to pretend that we didn't. And I can still see Jennifer's face, looking up at me, waiting for answers I could not give then, and in many ways cannot give now.

I more often than not see only dusty, empty rooms when I search that place of my past where my mind sometimes wanders but rarely lingers. I believe in words like psychosis, endogenous depression, addiction, and bipolar disorder, and I believe in neurochemical imbalances and "bad wiring" of the brain. I can spout lots of technical jargon and use psychoanalytical language to describe some things science understands and some things it does not.

I'm supposed to have some understanding of neurotransmitters and receptor molecules, but all that can't completely explain how people sometimes become lost to themselves and lost to the rest of us. And somewhere inside myself, I believe in unseen darkness and demons, too, and on any given day, depending on how my own neurotransmitters happen to be firing or misfiring, I'm not at all sure where one set of beliefs leaves off and the other takes up.

After so many years in my own recovery, sometimes all I can cling to is a knowing deep within me that God exists, that there is a world beyond what we can see and touch and feel, and that within that world evil exists, too. And I believe that for some of us in obvious ways, and probably all of us in more subtle ways, the disease exists and makes its home in more than just our flesh, and medicine alone rarely cures us.

When all my training fails me, all I really know for sure is that being well—truly well—goes to a place within us that lies far deeper than the mere molecules that make us up, and that for whatever reasons, my mother, my sister, and I, all of us at different times, began to fall away, isolated, staring out from our own internal windows at the intruding gray, mourning something lost that none of us could find.

I could not rescue my mother and sister. I should have known better. I counsel people all the time about it, telling them to let go, to hand over their loved ones to the only One who ever saves any of us.

The truth is, in recent days I've wondered if I could continue the fight. I have felt, if not beaten, at least emptied. I have felt, honestly, that I can't help myself anymore, much less those people who come every day for my counsel. I can't listen to any more pain. I can't walk another step in the darkness.

Yet this time, as this merciless disease has stolen yet another loved one from my life, some thirty years since my mother's death, *something* has been different. This time, I have not struggled as much in my soul with the crushing feelings of guilt and self-blame. This time, I have looked into a lifeless face and seen both tragedy and great beauty, where three decades ago I saw only loss. This time, when lightly brushing my fingertips against a cold, colorless cheek, I have felt the overpowering truth that crushes death with nothing less than eternal life. Not an end, but a beginning.

I see that if I am to reach beyond my brokenness, I will have to rely on that most incomprehensible of things, a gift both beyond me and within me, a power called faith. Faith that God is in the rain, the pain, the loving and losing, the hurt and healing, the sun and the storm. Faith that God's hand is on both birth and death, love and loss, joy and tragedy, compulsion and cure, laughter and tears. Faith when prayers are answered and when they are not. Faith when the God of all giving inexplicably takes away. Faith that He longs to kiss the face of both the angel and the addict.

Faith that he is with me when I feel so helplessly alone. Faith that no matter how many times I turn my back on him, he is forever facing me.

Goodbye, Jennifer.
I have faith now.
I'll see you soon.

26

CHRISTOPHER ALLEN

Selma, Going On

"Made the cover of *Time*, the eighth of April, 1966," Selma said, slipping the wedding dress over her wizened shoulders. She always starved herself the month before the anniversary, just to make sure it still fit. "Lord, it's a hot day for a wedding." She pinned the graying veil into her white hair and turned to Hank. "This time he'll come. You'll see."

Hank raised his eyes to Selma and stared. He'd heard it all before.

A stained-glass Noah's Ark, hanging from a hook on the porch, magnified the morning sun and laser-licked the living room with searing rays of gold and scarlet.

Selma and Hank waited for Elroy, roasting in the carmine cathedral of the living room. When they couldn't bear the heat any longer, they retreated to the back of the farmhouse, to the royal-blue-tiled kitchen where Selma could at least keep an eye on Elroy's picture over the sink while she waited.

"Jesus. He's a looker," she said, pouring Hank some water from the tap. "I don't know how you drink this. It's just as warm as the dickens." She placed the water in front of him, sighed, gathered the wedding dress in her lap, and plopped down in the cool, vinyl kitchenette chair. "It's like he's here, but he ain't. Like God," she went on, as was her habit. For Selma, waiting for Elroy to come back was a hush that needed filling.

"More? Peas in a pod, Elroy and you. Elroy could drink the spring dry. Like glue, you two. My Word, Hank and Elroy..."

Hank had been close to Elroy until the second Elroy collapsed on the hill that evening, falling face down in the mud. Three strokes and he was gone.

"... Ought to be a law against it. You remember that time you and Elroy were standing outside the old shed? Elroy was building a chair and just talking up a storm," Selma cried. "And he told me *I* could talk the paint off the walls. Law me! But I reckon that's why he spent all his time with you." Selma waited for a reaction that didn't come. "Lord, won't Elroy think it's funny to see us together? Mercy me." She had to smile at life's little ironies. "Well, I remember his voice..."

And late into the afternoon, Selma went on. The dimming light in the kitchen and the fragrance of the blooming wild grapevines that crept over the house meant it was suppertime. She knew that Hank, who was now snoring on the three-seater in the living room, would have liked nothing better than a hamburger or steak, but he was on a strict diet.

"Sure would like to know what Elroy was saying that day." She mused at Elroy's velvet eyes in the picture. Like a handsome stranger, she thought. But Elroy *had* promised to marry her, hadn't he?

"I mean, what was so important that he got the itch to talk all of a sudden?" The question was meant more for Elroy's wide-eyed Jesus stare than for Hank. "I don't reckon he ever put ten words together to say Hoodoo to me. Just 'woman, do this' and 'woman, don't do that.' Law me, Hank. Hank?"

Selma dried her biggish hands on her dress and glanced over at Hank. "Are you listening to me?" she shouted loud enough to jolt him off the couch.

"You remember that day, Hank," she went on, as Hank staggered groggily into the kitchen. "Lord, honey, just grunt if you're still alive. I know you remember that day. I was in the house primping—I was gonna be such a handsome bride—and Elroy was at the shed with you. I ain't blaming you." She wiped a stain off the picture with the veil. "Never looks me in the eye," she said matter-of-factly.

"I reckon," she went on, "if we talked more . . . or maybe if I lived better . . . Lord, I don't know." She had to cackle at herself. The sound of laughter always made the waiting easier.

"Elroy has a beautiful voice. Like Moses in that Moses movie. If I'd known he was gonna go like that, I'd have taped that voice with that contraption Gayle gave me for my birthday. Probably would've just been something like 'Awh, go on and git that thang out of my face, woman! Go on!' But I'd have it, wouldn't I, Hank? And it would be Elroy on there talking to me. Imagine that!

"Elroy walked right up that hill and fell with them arms outstretched, hugging me one last time. I know I should've stayed in the house, but I came running out anyway all dressed up," she said, smoothing the frayed lace around her bosom.

" 'Is he dead? Is he dead?' I kept shouting, but no one was around except you. I ain't blaming you," Selma said too harshly and went back to preparing Hank's dinner. "Wish I'd had that cassette machine ready."

Selma stared out the window through a curtain of wild grapevines. Deep down, she wondered if Elroy weren't really dead. But Elroy had promised to marry her, she thought, and stared and thought some more until the emptiness needed filling again. Still staring out the window, she sang, " 'And He walks with me, and He talks with me, and He tells me I am His own. And the voice I hear, fall—' " but the voice stuck firmly in her throat. Lost in a past that was late coming back to her, she felt a little silly for putting on the wedding dress again. But then she had to laugh at herself. How wonderful! The resolute echo of laughter.

"But we go on, don't we, Hank? And ain't it funny: till Elroy comes back, at least I got someone to talk to in the meantime," she said and put Hank's bowl down on the cool linoleum. "Now, you go on and eat." Selma sighed and petted him on the head. "Oh, me. Even made the cover . . ."

ALANA WHITE

The Cloths of Heaven

Had I the heavens' embroidered cloths,
Enwrought with golden and silver light,
The blue and the dim and the dark cloths
Of night and light and the half light,
I would spread the cloths under your feet:
But I, being poor, have only my dreams;
I have spread my dreams under your feet;
Tread softly because you tread on my dreams.
   ["Aedh Wishes for the Cloths of Heaven"
   by William Butler Yeats, 1899]

Rosalee—who used to be vivacious and the life of the party, when she was in love, that is, before Raymond split for L.A., taking with him his electric keyboard and a big chunk of her heart—Rosalee stands at the door of the bedroom closet, feeling edgy, and stares at the clothes on the rack. In the dim recesses hang thigh-high skirts and stretchy tops in fruity colors like orange, strawberry, and peach. Last year's bridesmaid dress is scarlet with a black cummerbund.

A priest's ordination? Good Lord. In Rosalee's twenty-four years, she has never been near a priest, let alone gone to an ordination for one. Right now, she would like to phone Mary Lou and say she wants to curl on the couch in a faded T-shirt and watch *Lost* reruns, but that would leave Mary Lou high and dry on Friday night, and since Raymond's zippy departure last autumn, Rosalee has a new policy: if you can possibly help it, never disappoint anyone.

She tosses a yellow and brown blouse onto the bed alongside the jeans and Shania T-shirt she wore to the music studio today. She yanks the iron from beneath the bed, wipes its cobwebby bottom along the hip of her bikini panties, and pads to the dresser. The lingerie drawer is a mess—skimpy bras looped through camisole straps, teddies in a tangle. From beneath the underwear, she unearths a pair of cotton sweatpants. Hot Yoga. What in God's name had she been thinking? You keep yourself looking good for a man and does he appreciate it? Hell, no. She tosses the sweats back into the drawer and wanders naked into the bathroom, where she fills the tub and scoots back against the smooth white porcelain, feeling better as her skin tingles with warmth. Not *great*, but better.

"Heavens, girl, you just now getting ready?"

Rosalee yelps, so startled by Mary Lou's presence in the apartment she splashes up in the water like a fish.

"Sorry." Mary Lou's smirk says the opposite.

Before moving to Nashville, Mary Lou managed the gift shop at Graceland in Memphis. Now she works at the Country Music Hall of Fame and Museum here in town. Her blue-black hair is pouffy, her pencil-thin eyebrows plucked into high black arches.

"It's okay," Rosalee answers, but her heart is racing from being surprised like that.

"You wearing brown?" Mary Lou casts an appraising glance at the clothes on Rosalee's bed. Mary Lou has on the low-cut, parrot-green and orange sundress with kicky pleats she bought for a cruise to Jamaica last summer. Rosalee figures a priest's ordination for something like a baptism in her own church: a serious occasion. From what Mary Lou has told her, that flowered dress she is wearing tonight witnessed a host of shipboard activities that were anything but.

"Brown and yellow," Rosalee answers, toweling her curly hair.

Thinking of the Cathedral of the Incarnation, she imagines shadowy corners, flickering candles, and the dry rustling of priests' robes. Cassocks, Mary Lou calls them.

"Father Andy's entering the priesthood, he's not being buried," Mary Lou grumbles as she heats the iron. Glancing at her watch, she adds, "Have you eaten supper?"

Rosalee blows her nose—Nashville in April gives her allergies fits. "I had some Sour Cream Rancheros at noon." She doesn't eat much anymore. There is nothing she really wants.

The cathedral is nothing like the God Is Love Baptist Church back home in Lyon County, Kentucky. The pink and cream sanctuary, awash in late afternoon sunlight pouring through stained-glass windows, is delicate, as luscious as a wedding cake. Rosalee cranes her neck, admiring the vaulted ceiling painted in creamy shades of gold, aqua blue, and pink. Mary Lou's strappy high heels click across the marble floor as she and Rosalee approach the church front. They slide into a pew. A priest stands alone on the altar speaking words that echo high in the air. As if by magic, another priest materializes at his side. Rosalee knows this is Father Andy, not because he is young, with hair clipped short as a Ft. Campbell soldier's, but because he moves as if he is in a dream.

People cough and clear their throats all during the ordination ceremony. They stand up and sit down and kneel on narrow leather-padded benches. Rosalee digs a crumpled tissue from her shoulder bag and blows her nose as inconspicuously as possible, but the blond fellow across the aisle, the one who is on his knees and ought to be praying, looks at her and winks.

Rosalee glances away. While Mr. Flirt-in-Church is cute, no way is he as cute as Raymond, with his hair in a ponytail and eyes as sweet and soft as a doe's. No one is—but talk about jealous! Raymond had a fit if she just looked at another guy. Marrying him—following him to California—would have been like crouching at a starting line: bang! A pistol shot, and Rosalee Jane Talley would have been running for the rest of her life.

"We're invited to the reception," Mary Lou announces as they file with the congregation onto the concrete sidewalk. Automobiles speed along West End Avenue in both directions. Though now it is early evening, the April sky is sunny, a thin, watery blue with magenta bruises off toward the west.

In the car Mary Lou promises, "You'll love Father Andy."

Rosalee doubts it. She can't imagine being chummy with a priest. In her mind, priests inhabit a secret, soft place. "Cut from another cloth," as her mother would have put it.

Turning across traffic, Mary Lou drives away from downtown, saying, "Romeo ever send the money he owes?"

Romeo. "Yes," Rosalee answers—a tiny white lie.

Mary Lou inhales, really enjoying that Virginia Slim. "Great! Panama City, here we come."

Rosalee's toes scrunch in the tips of her brown flats. She has never been to the beach. She's wary of the Gulf of Mexico. She is not a swimmer. On Animal Planet she has heard about jellies, stingrays, and sharks. Mary Lou will insist, will goad her into the water. Gulf. The word says it all.

By the time they reach the KC Club, which Mary Lou says means "Knights of Columbus," the party room is noisy with Catholics drinking champagne. Viewing Father Andy up close, Rosalee notices how his eyes glisten because he is so happy. He embraces his guests. He embraces Rosalee, his crisp white cassock smelling pleasantly of Niagara Starch. "Have some cake," he says. "Have some champagne."

Mary Lou accepts a glass. Laughing—the bubbles tickle her nose—she tells Father Andy she will see him at Mass Saturday afternoon, then starts through the jostling crowd toward a sea of tables and metal folding chairs. "Be there in a minute," Rosalee says over Father Andy's chattering guests.

At the bar she orders a Corona with a slice of lime and, Lord, it tastes good. On the far side of the room, Mary Lou lounges, head thrown back, enjoying the company of two guys in suits, white shirts, and dark ties who have joined her at a table. Rosalee goes over, thinking, Damn it, and draws back, startled.

"Hey!" says the blond fellow who caught her blowing her nose in church. "You must be Rosalee." Blondie's name is Bob. His friend is Julian somebody.

"Bob and Julian are in the seminary," Mary Lou says, practically shivering with delight.

Well, there's a relief. From Mary Lou, Rosalee has heard all about that vow of chastity.

The four of them talk, drinking beer and champagne, Mary Lou blowing blue cigarette smoke toward the ceiling fan. Julian keeps checking his watch: a friend driving from out of state is late arriving. When at last a fellow in a rumpled blue shirt and wrinkled khakis walks into the club, Julian pops up. "Morris!"

Near the tiered cake decorated with white frosting and the punch bowl where scoops of orange sherbet are drowning in 7UP, Julian slaps Morris on the back. They laugh it up with Father Andy, then stroll to the jam-packed bar and pick up five beers before coming to the table. Judging from the bear hug Bob gives Morris, Bob, too, thinks a lot of the guy. Both fellows do. They fall over themselves making introductions, getting Morris settled—in the chair beside Rosalee, in fact.

Morris is pretty average. His hair is short, but not as short as Father Andy's. His suntanned face is plain. He wouldn't win any prizes for neatness, either, Rosalee thinks. Mud cakes the soles of his Nikes and the hem of his pants.

"Morris," Julian says. "What happened? You missed the ceremony."

Morris lifts one shoulder. "The van had a flat. In the middle of a raging storm, for a little extra drama." His eyes gleam with mischief. "When I got back inside, I didn't want to ruin the upholstery, so I took off my pants and shirt. That's when the policewoman pulled up."

Blond Bob bursts into laughter. Julian frowns. "You're making this up."

"Swear to God, I'm not." Morris sets down his beer. "I'm lucky she didn't arrest me."

Bob grins. "For what? Disappointment?" He and Mary Lou tap their beer bottles together, and Rosalee can't help but laugh. Even sourpuss Julian cracks a smile. There is something about Morris that Rosalee likes. Something devilish beats beneath that cottony blue shirt.

"So, Morris, how's the cheese business?" Julian says.

"Going strong. We filled a ton of orders for Christmas. I mean literally."

"They make a lot of cheese in Kentucky?" Rosalee says. "Wow. I didn't know that, and I'm from there."

"Where?" he says.

"Lyon County."

"Ah. The penitentiary. Well, in Bardstown, they do. Make a lot of cheese, that is." He sets his empty beer bottle on the table and smiles straight at her.

This guy is no Brad Pitt, but his eyes are a bright shade of blue. When he smiles, they crinkle at the corners, and Morris smiles a lot. Rosalee glances away and inspects her fingernails, wishing she hadn't bitten them to the quick.

"You live in Nashville now?" he says.

Rosalee nods and tells him she works for Russell Outlaw Music, which, of course, publishes country songs. Meanwhile, Mary Lou and the two seminarians are talking shop across the

THE CLOTHS OF HEAVEN

table. A lot of Father Andy's friends have switched to martinis with olives, and the KC Club is louder by the second. Naturally, Morris scoots closer to Rosalee.

"I like classical," he says. "Do you?" He props his cheek in his hand, his eyes fixed on her. "You look like someone who might."

Her skin tingles. She feels an attraction to him that comes out of the blue. Lips pursed, Julian looks over and, after a moment, glances away.

Classical? Rosalee thinks. Last October, she and Raymond and two other couples had iced down three coolers of beer and driven Raymond's van into the Smoky Mountains, to a chalet in the pines. Early one morning when she couldn't sleep, she had wandered onto the balcony in a T-shirt. The sun was rising like a big orange ball over the mountains, and as if that wasn't enough, from one of the cabins on the hillside there came the sound of a fiddle and a Dobro playing, and that music was so pure, she thought she would weep—till Raymond stepped outside, singing, "When all at once a mighty herd of red-eyed cows I saw," and goosed her ribs with a cold bottle of Bud.

Before Rosalee can give Morris the right answer, Bob says, "Hey, why don't we all go dancing?"

It's unusually hot for April, Rosalee thinks once they are outside. In the night sky, heat lightning flickers, and they feel a drizzle of rain. The guys decide they will drive Bob's beat-up Toyota downtown to the Wildhorse Saloon. Later, they will bring Morris back by the Catholic club for his van. "I never realized priests like to party," Rosalee says to Morris while the details are worked out. "So, how do you know Bob and Julian?"

"School. St. Louis," he says, smiling. "But I left there two years ago."

Yes! Thank you, God, she thinks, beaming as she climbs into Mary Lou's front seat. In silence, they drive back down

West End Avenue past the dark cathedral toward the Nashville riverfront in misting rain, Bob's headlights bouncing along behind them, Rosalee thinking she has not felt so happy in a long time. At least, not since that jerk Ray took off. Morris is nice. Morris is smart, and he likes her but doesn't let his eyes flick down toward her breasts. Well, maybe once.

At the Saloon, he sits beside her again. Huge speakers blare country music, and on the hardwood floor couples take free dance lessons. "Quite a place," Morris shouts over the music.

"There is this classical song I like," she shouts back.

"Can't hear you." He pulls his chair closer.

"I don't know the title." She hums the tune, her heart going wild again.

"Pachebel!" he says. "A terrific seventeenth-century composer. German."

And she says, "They play it on this infomercial on TV."

He scribbles the name of the tune on the back of a white paper napkin with a turquoise and red horse printed on it, and she puts the napkin in her purse, considering at the same time how weird it is that some song from hundreds of years ago is on a television commercial today. Well. That's one way to keep from paying royalties.

When Mary Lou and Morris's buddies squeeze onto the dance floor and do the two-step—Brooks & Dunn, Reba and Vince, they do it all—Rosalee finds herself telling Morris about her family. When she was fourteen, her mother died the morning she drove a mile to the grocery store for milk and a deer crashed through her windshield, causing the pickup to fly off the highway. Leaving her dad and moving to Nashville two years ago was hard for Rosalee. (She does not mention her Aunt Gaynelle, who was featured in the Nashville newspaper after being taken aboard a spaceship in Bowling Green, Kentucky, and released after being thoroughly examined.)

The Saloon is warm with tourists dancing. Perspiration

THE CLOTHS OF HEAVEN

trickles along Rosalee's spine. It drips between her breasts. She fans her brown and yellow blouse. She is feeling ripe. Cheerfully, she tells the waitress, "We'd like a pizza, large, deep dish," and orders a club soda. Morris switched from beer to water after they left the club.

When he was a boy, he says, he dreamed he would be a photographer. In Africa, filming wild leopards and lions.

Her heart is beating fast. She lifts her hair, lets it fall, tries to look away from him, and can't. He's not tall, like the other guys she has dated. He doesn't have a snappy twinkle in his eyes, like Raymond. And yet his mouth is full and ready. His calloused hands are wide and tanned and strong. She admires those tough fingers turned up on the table and wonders what they would do to her skin.

Cheeks burning, she says, "You mean like the photographers on Animal Planet where they turn bright lights on in the middle of the night, and the animals are all so startled?" The cats' copper eyes flash before they melt into the jungle shadows. She has always admired those fearless tigers and lions and even the hyenas, with their glittering eyes and sloping backs. They are ready for *anything*; don't doubt it for a minute.

"Well, yes," he says, his face startled. "Exactly like that. I think."

Smiling, Rosalee wipes pizza sauce from her mouth and takes another slice of the pie, scooting over for Mary Lou and the guys, who look beat from all that dancing. "Morris," Julian says, his voice sharp as he glances at Rosalee. "I've been meaning to ask you how the garden is doing."

"Fine." Morris shrugs. "This year we planted outside the walls."

"Outside the walls?" Rosalee laughs, but feels her stomach dip. "What are you, on parole?" Inside her chest, her heartbeat slows.

Without a moment's hesitation, Bob says, "No, he's a monk."

"What?" She smiles as if this could be a joke, when she already knows it is not. Morris is a monk. Lightly, she says, "I always thought monks wore robes with hoods and ropes tied around their waists." Not khakis. Not cottony, eye-matching blue shirts.

Smiling lazily, Mary Lou says, "What *do* you wear, Morris?"

"A robe with a hood and a rope belt tied around my waist." He removes his arm from the back of Rosalee's chair, his face solemn as he glances over at Julian and Bob.

"This," Rosalee says, "is interesting."

"There's an understatement," Mary Lou says. "Morris, you're at Gethsemane? That is so cool. Maybe sometime Rosalee and I can come on a retreat."

He nods yes and his monk's eyes linger on Rosalee, who feels as if she has slipped down into a full bathtub and is hearing this conversation under water. Big smiles wreathe Julian and Bob's faces.

Rosalee says, "What do you do there? Besides hoe and make cheese?"

"Pray. Work. Pray some more," Morris says, subdued.

The lamps of automobiles cruising Second Avenue illuminate the pavement in wavy ribbons of light. Before climbing into the car—Mary Lou guns the engine—Rosalee pauses, looking over her shoulder at Brother Morris. He is standing with one hand on the door of Bob's Toyota, watching her with eyes so dark and troubled, they steal her breath away. It lasts one moment only, but she feels a conversation take place between them.

Are you okay with this?

What a question, Morris. Should I be?

He has moved one step toward her when she turns away.

The street where she lives is dark and quiet, the houses asleep beneath a moon impossibly round and white. In silence, she slips through the grass toward the wrought-iron steps leading to her apartment. She feels like one of those good-looking cats caught in the jungle with a light shining on it. She is feeling giddy. She is feeling good, like yesterday's Rosalee. She feels like shouting, "I'm beautiful. Go ahead—look at me." Hurrying up the steps, she considers Mary Lou's travel brochures. She considers the Florida panhandle, with its burning sun, sugary white sand, and emerald waters so wide, they are a full embrace. Tomorrow, she will call her daddy.

"Florida?" he will say, like she is taking a trip to Egypt. "What'll you do there, girl?"

"Eat fish, Daddy. Swim," she will answer, surprising him again.

MARY ANN WEAKLEY

Face of a Nun

The harsh clang of the antique school bell reverberated in the distant halls until it reached the doorway of the fourth-floor convent dormitory where I slept. Sister Edmund, the bell-ringer, must have slept in her habit to be dressed and ready to ring that bell before dawn. Her rumpled, thrown-together appearance suggested that. Her veil always fell a little cockeyed over what once was a precisely pleated white coif around her face.

I always loved being up in the early mornings. I just never enjoyed *getting* up. At home, I would have hit the clock's snooze button, but now there was no snooze alarm on the simple wooden nightstand beside my narrow bed. No clock at all.

Miss Mary, a reliable postulant, flipped the light switch at the door and shattered the last speck of the night's serenity. As the only novice in the dorm, I should have been the one to rise quickly and turn on the lights as a model for the younger postulants. I was expected to lead by example. Procrastination was not an admirable trait in a nun. Habitual procrastination was tantamount to sin in a convent.

My reluctant feet hit the cold hardwood floor that October morning. My knees bent down for a "Good Morning, God" prayer. I leaned against the bed, smothered my face in my hands, and turned my prayerful thoughts to God. For a moment, I thought I detected a strangeness in my face.

Like a nest of birds fluttering their wings in the quiet of daybreak, the dormitory rustled with the movement of postulants dressing in morning silence. Sitting on the straight wooden chair next to my bed, I pulled on black opaque stockings and rolled them down to just below the knees, giving them a twist into a knot. The long, straight, one-size-fits-all blue cotton slip slid over my head and narrow young shoulders and fell almost to the floor. Modestly wrapped in my robe, toothbrush and toothpaste in hand, I drew back the white curtain around my cell and made my way to the common washroom just outside the dormitory.

My white towel and washcloth hung first in rank on the towel bar that stretched across the wall from corner to corner above the sinks. My MAC initials were stitched in red on the towel edges, as it appeared on all of my clothing for identification purposes in the laundry. In the land of anonymity, that simple mark displayed the rare evidence of personal possession. Those initials were a reminder of who I was before I became Sister Mary Magdalen.

I moved zombie-like around the washroom, then took my turn at the sink. I rubbed my hand over my face. There was a slight tightness on the left side. The annoyance prompted a spontaneous urge to look in a mirror. There was no mirror, of course. The natural instinct was to study my face, not out of vanity, but out of curiosity. Even if tempted to vanity, there was little to be vain about. Everyone wore the same clothing style, our hair didn't show, and we never wore makeup. Regardless of the rule of morning silence, I was tempted to ask Miss Carol, a postulant, to look at my face. But there was no time as we rushed to dress for chapel.

Piece by piece I put on my religious habit, a ritual still new to me. The white veil was pinned to the white band—starched board-stiff and folded into a squared shape over my forehead. I empathized with Sister Edmund for having to get all this garb on and ring the bell by five, and I wouldn't blame her if she did sleep in her habit.

Four months prior, I received the habit at the Reception Ceremony. From the beginning I doubted I would ever get all eight pieces on straight and make it to the chapel in time for morning prayers. At least there was no time-consuming decision on what to wear.

I had all but forgotten my facial sensation through morning prayers, Mass, and meditation. No one gave me a strange look. Actually no one looked at anyone. The proper posture for nuns, especially novices, was to keep our eyes down. Gawking around was considered a distraction to our thoughts, as well as to others.

I was already schooled in that practice. My mother, by her example, had taught me the proper demeanor in church. She could correct me with only a frown if I was gawking around. I don't mean to say we didn't share a nudge and a grin now and then, like when Mrs. Wallace made her predictable last-minute entrance before Mass swaying to and fro with heavy strides to the very front pew. Her long mink coat trailed behind her like a bridal train. Without the slightest turn of her head from the altar, Mother would give me an elbow punch in the ribs with a guarded smile that said, "Hold your laugh till later."

Sister Sheila and I were scheduled to serve breakfast to the Sisters in the dining room. After Mass and before meditation, we left the chapel to dash with decorum down the stairs to the basement dining room where we were assigned to set up the table servings.

Breakfast was the easiest meal to serve, even while keeping the required silence. Sister Sheila and I had learned the ropes in our first year as postulants. We could do it blindfolded. With flowing white veils tied back and bib-front long white aprons pinned on, we rushed around the institutional kitchen, stacking toast on plates as it fell from the rotating toaster and pulling butter cubes from the walk-in cooler, placing them on serving plates. We passed cereal-filled bowls, cream pitchers, and jelly dishes to the tables, six Sisters to a serving. By the time the coffee pots were filled and ready for pouring, the other Sisters filed silently down the stairs and lined up like dominoes while they waited for the signal to be seated at the long refectory tables in the painted white cinder-block basement room. Everyone ate in silence as one of the Sisters read from *The Lives of the Saints*.

Only after Sister Sheila and I finished clearing dishes, put food away, and cleaned up, could we sit down to our breakfast. While washing the serving dishes in the shallow trough-like sink, I sensed the tightness again.

"Do you see anything wrong with my face?" I whispered to Sister Sheila.

With a quick glance and a shake of her head, she whispered, "No, nothing."

I put on a big smile and said, "Look again."

Silence was broken. "Oh, my gosh! Magdalen, what is wrong with you? One side of your face is frozen!" She pushed me off to see the nurse.

Sister Bernarda, the convent nurse, wore an all-white habit and veil. Her office was a three-by-five-foot dispensary, halfway down the third-floor infirmary hall.

I waited my turn behind senior-ranking Sisters. Never an alarmist, Sister Bernarda spoke calmly, "Um hum, uh, smile again, dear."

She studied my face as she murmured reassurances. In my effort to smile again, I detected concern through her veiled calm. "What do you see?" I asked.

She handed me a mirror.

"What happened to my face?" I begged a simple explanation.

The left side was totally paralyzed. There was no movement when I smiled.

Sister Bernarda rang Sister Philomene, superior of novices, and put in a call to the doctor for advice and an appointment.

"Until I hear from the doctor, I think it would be best for you to go back to the dormitory and rest. No duties for you today."

I went to the dormitory and prepared for bed in the middle of the morning, the sun still shining. I pulled the white curtains across the rods to enclose my little cubicle. Confused, frightened, and exhausted, I fell asleep until Sister Sheila brought me lunch. After lunch my classmates came to cheer me up. They made me laugh so they could see the half-frozen face. Although I needed their silliness to relieve my anxiety, they couldn't hide their sudden shocked expressions.

The doctor prescribed vitamin B-complex shots and rest. But there was no definitive diagnosis. At nineteen, I was too young to consider stroke as the cause.

"It could be as simple as a draft on your face during the night, which would mean it's a temporary affliction," he said.

Even his ultimate assessment was tentative.

"From all indications and tests, it's probably Bell's palsy, a paralysis of the face, sometimes temporary, and possibly permanent," he said.

That was enough to scare me into strictly following his orders.

Bedrest in the isolated third-floor dormitory felt like a punishment. I neither felt nor looked sick, at least not until I smiled. Fear of permanent paralysis was beginning to set in. After a couple of days of restful sleep, I expected to see improvement. But there was none, and as the second week began, I started to panic. The left side showed signs of drawing.

To occupy my time, I read the lives of the saints between frequent naps and visits from the nurse. If it had been permissible, I would have passed time writing letters. There was little to do but read, sleep, worry, and pray. Saying the prayers of the rosary occupied my mind. My fingers passed over the beads as I repeated a Hail Mary—at each bead, petitioning the Mother of God to intercede with her Son on my behalf.

My anxiety increased as the next weekend approached. My parents were scheduled to make their first visit since Reception Day in June, the day I had received the habit and became a novice. What if I were not back to normal by then? As eager as I was to see them, I didn't want them to be alarmed by my tragedy-comedy face. My father had already suffered two paralyzing strokes, and I didn't want the sight of my face to cause the third.

On the day of their visit, I had been dressed and ready since morning Mass at 6:30. When Sister Philomene came to announce that they had arrived, I walked slowly from the novitiate quarters down the wide hardwood hall toward the large guest parlor, anticipating the fear I would see in my parents' eyes when they saw my face.

I made an effort to bounce into the room with some semblance of my usual joy. For a brief moment I was able to camouflage the distortion in my face with tears of happiness at the first sight of them. They rose in unison from the stiff formal Victorian parlor chairs to greet me with hugs.

Though warned that I was not feeling well, they were devastated at the sight of my half-smile. After a warm embrace, my father held me back at arm's length to examine my face. I caught the familiar scent of his cigar, a smell I normally disliked, but now it was a comforting smell of home. Mother was dressed in her Sunday best. As I hugged her, I could feel her posture slump a bit from her stately carriage. Though she bravely tried to maintain an upbeat conversation, the cracking in her voice and the quiver of her lips betrayed her concern.

"Don't worry, Mom, I'll get better. It's probably only temporary."

"You can still eat, can't you?" My dad pulled a Mounds candy bar out of his jacket pocket, remembering the favorite bar he would always bring home to me when I was little.

They examined me over and over, hoping for my complete smile to show up. I suspected my father feared that I'd had a type of stroke. It was a natural first assumption because of his previous strokes and the history of heart conditions in his family.

My father could look very official and intimidating when dressed in his Sunday three-piece suit in contrast to his farm work-clothes. He pressed for an answer from Sister Philomene.

"What is being done to correct her condition?"

"She is resting and taking shots prescribed by the doctor." Sister Bernarda spoke up with her calm voice, explaining the Bell's palsy.

That was not a sufficient explanation for him. He was used to fixing things for me. Bowing to the nuns who were now in charge of my life was crippling to his style.

He grew quieter as the weekend progressed. I knew he was regretting my decision to become a nun while still in my teens. I had been home from boarding school only three months before leaving again for the convent. He had wanted me to wait at least a year to make sure of my decision.

We had a mutual admiration for each other. He still carried my baby picture in his wallet, and had always granted my every wish for the pleasure of my smile. I had always known I could get what I wanted from him, but I was sensible enough not to push for the ridiculous. Often, I'd first take a cue from my mother as to what would fly with him, or whether it was a good day to ask. It hurt me now to see the anguish on his face.

At the end of the weekend I walked them to their car and kissed them goodbye. The tears in my father's eyes conveyed his heavy heart. Mother struggled to smile as she said goodbye.

"Get your rest and follow the doctor's orders, Toots. I'll be praying hard."

I had no doubt that when my mother talked to God, He listened. I watched as they drove down the gravel driveway, then turned toward home and the four-hour drive. My heart was breaking for them. I welcomed the isolation of bedrest as I pulled the curtains around my sparsely appointed cubicle and curled up in a tight ball.

I rested in the days and weeks that followed. Eventually, I persuaded Sister Bernarda that my energy was coming back. The alone time was wearing on me. I could only do so much reading, and I hadn't yet mastered the art of praying constantly. Home was often on my mind. I wondered how my parents were handling the lack of information.

With coaxing, Sister Bernarda allowed me to go to Mass and to meals, but I was not to participate in any physical work activity. No cleaning, no dishes, no gardening, no serving at meals.

At my daily check-ins with Sister Bernarda, I heard reports of gradual progress. My face was less drawn, and there was a slight crook of a smile. I was beginning to believe the paralysis might leave my face for good. Vitamins and prayers were working.

In early December, ten weeks after it struck me, the paralysis was gone.

By Christmas, I was well again and back to normal. There were multiple reasons to celebrate. My parents' next visit was scheduled just after New Year's. They learned through Sister Philomene my paralysis was gone.

As visiting day drew close, I was anticipating a joyous reunion. After lunch that Sunday when Sister Philomene called me to the parlor, I practically ran, or I would have if such behavior were permitted. I bounced into the parlor with joy in my heart and on both sides of my face.

"Merry Christmas!" I beamed the smile they had longed to see. "And Happy New Year!"

We chattered about everything. They shared the news from home about my brothers, my girlfriend's engagement, and my dog Mickey. They told me of their plans for a Florida trip in late January. Now that I was well, they felt they could go ahead as planned and take their first extended winter vacation to Ft. Myers. My father's doctor had given him an all-clear sign at his recent check-up. They were looking forward to rest and relaxation.

I soaked up the smell of my father's cigar to remember until the next visit. When the evening prayer bell rang, it signaled time for them to leave and for me to go to chapel. We slowly walked arm in arm down the familiar hallway to the front door where I gave each of them a long, tight hug and wished them a great vacation. A satisfied expression of contentment was on my father's face. There were happy tears in the corners of his eyes.

Mother blew me a kiss from the car as they turned down the gravel driveway. At the last turn, my father looked back and gave me a smile and a final wave as he pulled out a cigar for the road.

He'd finally accepted that I was in good hands and happy with my life. He knew he no longer needed to protect me.

Just four weeks after I saw them, they were enjoying several days in the Florida sun. After a morning at the beach, my father walked to a nearby tourist store in search of cigars. As he returned, headed toward their beach cottage, he was stricken with a heart attack. He died alone on the sidewalk of Ft. Myers Beach.

I remembered our last goodbye—it was the final separation from my protector.

29

SUSIE DUNHAM

The Cowboy Tie

My dad was an accordion player in a cowboy band in upstate New York. They practiced in our parlor, where I'd hide in a corner and listen to them until I fell asleep. The next morning I would wake up in my bed with the foggy memory of music and smiling men. I'm pretty sure those nights were filled with the best sleep a little girl could get.

When Daddy was going out for a job with his band, he'd dress up in his good black pants (also worn for weddings and funerals), a long-sleeved plaid shirt with cowboy stitching on the pockets, and a splash of Old Spice. The piece that completed the outfit was a black clip-on Western bow tie with long tails. His cowboy tie. It set off his outfit and made him the most handsome dad in the world.

Well, even the most handsome, cowboy-tie-wearing dads die. I lost him in 1988. He was sixty-two.

For eighteen years he would come intermittently to my mother in her sleep, hold his hand out to her, and plead with her to go with him. She'd shoo him away and tell him, "Go back. I'm not ready yet." During a night in September of 2006, he must have visited her again. She was tired and knew she was not going to win her battle with pulmonary fibrosis. When he reached out to her, she gladly took his hand. She was seventy-seven.

We drove home to New York from Tennessee for Mom's services. It was a little before three in the morning when we stopped for the night somewhere in Ohio. The hotel room was quiet and pitch black, which amplified thoughts of my mom as I tried to force myself to sleep. I lay on my side and faced the darkness. I'm not sure if my eyes were opened or closed when I saw my parents holding hands. I do know, however, that I found sleep.

As the first-year anniversary of Mom's passing approached, my sister was ready to face her toughest task. She had done some major projects in the small house she and Mom shared for forty-seven years and had weeded through tons of items our pack-rat mother had saved. Now she was ready to face our mother's bedroom. Sis cleaned out Mom's small dresser and emptied the bookcases. Totally overwhelmed by the memories in every drawer and on every shelf, she saved the armoire for me.

It had been almost a year since I'd been home. Seeing the changes to the house my sister had accomplished made me happy for her. She was making the house hers room by room. Not erasing Mom's presence, but creating her own. She was emotionally drained by the time I arrived. I assured her I could do this last sensitive task, and I prepared to face the stuffed armoire alone.

The top of the armoire was full of colorful and familiar winter sweaters, old and new, some with tags, some still in bags. Piled awkwardly in two columns, they looked as if they were in the process of being shuffled like a deck of cards. I removed a familiar blue sweater. She had bought me one in cream from her favorite store, QVC. I decided to take the blue sweater home and hang it in my closet. There are days when I lift the sleeve just to hold it close to my cheek.

Dozens of souvenir tee-shirts, collected over the decades from places the entire family had vacationed, were folded neatly in drawers. Places like Myrtle Beach, Maine, Lake George, and Cape Cod where Mom and Sis went every year at least twice. Even if Mom had been to a place multiple times, there was always a new shirt that had to be purchased to validate the vacation.

After a few false starts, I talked myself into a don't-look-at-them-just-move-them mentality. I had wasted time and energy by looking and crying. Now it was time to just get the job finished. So after emptying what seemed like hundreds of knit sweaters and thousands of Mom's much-loved cotton tees into the black holes of large garbage bags for Goodwill, I was down to emptying the last two drawers. One held unopened pantyhose that must have been bought twenty years ago, on sale, along with a few other unemotional items.

In the back of the second-to-last drawer, I poked my hand around and felt a stiff plastic bag. Money? Mom often thought her house was a safer place than a bank. I pulled the bag out from its dark, cramped hiding spot. The clouded bag, which was folded and rolled, wasn't heavy, and I wondered if there was anything in it at all. As I opened it, I noticed dark forms through the foggy plastic. What in the world had she saved in this old bag?

Deep in the bottom of the oversized opaque sack were two clip-on neckties from the 1960s—one sporting wide navy-blue and brown stripes accented with narrow stripes of red and white, the other featuring wide bands of dark blue and green. The wedding and funeral ties. Lying beneath the two familiar neckties was the cowboy tie—the tie that made my dad the most handsome dad in the world.

I held it in my hands and wept for my long-ago, easy childhood and for my mom who had saved that time in our lives when we were both in love with the parlor cowboy.

JIM TAULMAN

The Photograph

The package arrived wrapped in brown paper. My cousin had called me a few days earlier and told me it was on its way.

I ripped off the paper and opened the box inside. It was filled with centuries' worth of family "stuff" collected by my aunt who had died last year at 101.

I lifted out the items. Letters written a hundred and fifty years ago that contained correspondence between two cousins. Information on an ancient relative who had fought in the Revolutionary War. Tidbits on our family history my aunt had gleaned from various sources. Deeds to the last house my grandfather had owned. I was transported through history as I touched and read.

As I neared the bottom of the box, I saw it. It was small—about four inches by six, but two inches thick. It was a beautiful leather photo album stamped with gold foil. It looked to be at least a hundred and fifty years old. The bottom part of the clasp was missing, but otherwise it was in remarkable condition.

I opened the album and discovered that it was filled with small tintypes. The first photo was my great-grandfather. I had never seen a photo of him and did not even know that any such photo existed. But there was no mistaking that he was my great-grandfather. The gaunt face typical of my father, my uncle, and my grandfather stared out at me from the picture. The big protruding ears also linked him with my family and made me glad that I had escaped that part of my heritage.

He had an interesting set of chin whiskers. The rest of his face was clean-shaven, but from his chin, the whiskers extended six or seven inches. The ends of his moustache hung past the jaw line with pointed ends. This made him look like he was wearing an inverted V on his chin. His hair was close-cropped and combed straight back.

He had on a wide-lapel jacket made of some kind of soft material. Under that, he wore a vest and a white shirt that looked like a false front with a collar.

There he was. My great-grandfather. There was no date on the picture, but based on others in the album I guessed it must have been taken in 1870. If so, he would have been fifty. Had a traveling photographer taken this picture as a fiftieth birthday celebration? Or had the family gone to a studio and had the photograph made?

Who was this man who stared out at me from this ancient photograph?

I know so little about him. Hardly any stories have survived about this man to whom I owe my very existence.

Who was he?

I do know that he lived to be ninety-four—a long full life. He had three wives. The first one bore him all his children and then died in childbirth with what would have been their tenth child—a daughter. So I do know that he had a great desire for physical intimacy.

Who was this man?

Did he share the same feelings that I have—anger, love, selfishness, generosity, sadness, joy? What were his religious feelings? Was he a carouser, or was he quiet and mild-tempered? Did he enjoy telling a good joke and laughing? Was he able to communicate with his children and his wife? Were they afraid of him, or did they love him?

Who was this man who stared out at me?

Did he worry about making the payments on the farm? What did he do when the rains didn't come and he lost a crop? Did he have any money saved back for a rainy day, or did he live on the edge like most dirt farmers? How did he feel if ever his family went hungry?

Who was this man who stared out at me from this ancient photograph?

What skills did he possess? Could he build a piece of furniture that made people run their fingers over it admiringly? Or was he utilitarian, putting things together just to meet a particular need without any thought for beauty and fineness? Could he calm a frightened calf separated from its mother? Could he plant seeds and harvest a crop when others around him experienced crop failure?

Who was this man?

Could he read? If so, what did he read? What books were available to him? Many families on the frontier had a prized copy of the Bible. Did he have one? If so, did he read it? Beyond that, did he try to live by what he read? Did the family have other books? Had he gone to school? If so, what level had he attained?

Who was this man?

There are many specific bits of information I will never know about this man who stared out at me from this ancient photograph. Yet, there are many things I can know.

He bled when he cut his finger. He hurt when he hit his finger with a hammer. He cried—either externally or internally—when his wife and baby died. He hurt as he grew older and his body no longer was as lithe and supple as it had been in his younger days. He worried about caring for nine children.

I will never know all I would like to, but I can know a lot. For he is me, and I am him. He is bone of my bone and flesh of my flesh. Though separated by a century and a half, we are united in a way that I have yet to fathom.

Who is this man who stares out at me from this ancient photograph?

This man is me.

LINDA McCLURE DUNN

The Buttermilk Goblet

The side is broken out now. The piece lies in the bottom of the goblet waiting for me to make time to repair it. It had survived intact for who-knows-how-many years before it came to me. It is one of only two tangible remembrances of a grandmother I never knew very well.

My father had been her mid-life baby. She was past seventy when I was born—no doubt an anticlimactic event since a dozen other grandchildren preceded me. Several hundred miles separated my grandmother's home from ours. That distance was still somewhat formidable in the '40s and early '50s, before interstate highways and luxury cars were common.

My grandmother enjoyed long train rides around the country visiting her children, who were literally distributed from coast to coast, until her health intervened. Her inability to travel coupled with my father's always short, never predictable vacation periods meant that my time with her when I was old enough to retain memories was seldom and brief.

I do remember how, on our rare visits, she always drank her buttermilk from a particular goblet. She had only the one glass in that style—plain crystal with a ball like a big marble at the center of the stem. I can see her long, thin, gnarled fingers worrying with the glass as the family talked at her kitchen table.

My grandmother was a tiny woman, less than five feet tall, but she carried her square shoulders and square chin as if she were a giant. She seldom spoke of her past. It was from a newspaper interview she gave in her late 80s that our family learned how, after her father's death, she assumed the role of overseer of his farm and its workers. Her brothers were still just children, and rather than see the family land sold, she rose to the occasion. She was sixteen years old at the time. She could not have known then how strength in the face of loss and disappointment would be her life's hallmark.

Until she fulfilled her self-imposed obligation to her brothers, she delayed her marriage. A few years later, she lost one of her babies. Then, in the prime of life, her husband sickened and died, leaving her once again in charge of a farm. Nature took the farm during a short period of drought that foreshadowed the Dust Bowl. At age fifty my grandmother found herself with worthless land, no income, and three of her children still dependent on her. Though she shared little of these life events, even my child-self sensed their weight cloaking her. To me, she seemed both splendid and sad.

When she died, my father took her favorite goblet as a remembrance. There were few possessions for her six children to divide. After my father's death, I found the goblet in a closet in his house. Also there, carefully wrapped in a yellowing sheet, was a quilt top she had pieced. The quilt-in-progress was a surprise, as it was not like her to leave a project unfinished. I knew she had not been able to travel for twenty years prior to her death. Had she left the quilt at my parents' house thinking to complete it on her next visit? It would have been like her to assume there would be another visit, to deny the unpredictability Life attempted to force upon her. The goblet and the quilt top came home with me, to be stored away again for another generation to discover in their turn.

Sometimes when I noticed the goblet sitting at the back of my kitchen cabinet, I would ponder its significance to my grandmother. When she drank from it every day, did it remind her of the beloved husband with whom she had once shared a comfortable home? Was it perhaps the one fine possession remaining after Chance had robbed her of so much? When she had completed a day of the drudgery undertaken to sustain her family, was the goblet a magic talisman, briefly restoring memories of things lost? Only the goblet knows for sure.

Finally I put the goblet on my mantle where I could commune with it more easily. I foolishly allowed grandchildren to use it as a candy dish. One of them had an accident with it. I should have known it would happen. He and I both cried.

But now I wonder if there is symbolism in the breaking of the goblet. Perhaps in its shattered state the goblet is even more representative of my grandmother's shattered life, which somehow could never be mended: shards lovely in themselves but lacking form, surviving but without the ability to fulfill its potential, enduring but forever damaged.

32

GINGER MANLEY

Medical Miracles

"Grandma, can I hit your knee with my hand?" Alexander asked, as he perched beside me on the green canvas-covered swing seat on our back deck. Most every afternoon about five o'clock, he and Grandpa and I sat down with a mug of tea, or for Grandpa, a glass of wine, and a small treat to discuss the goings-on of the day. This was the third summer Alexander had traveled from his home in California to visit us in Tennessee.

Last year, he had had a serious meltdown the night he arrived. After bravely crawling into bed and hugging the tattered remnant of his baby blanket, he had found even this lovey could not replace his longing for his mommy and daddy and younger brother and sister.

"Please take me back to the airport, Grandma. My heart hurts," he pleaded, his big green eyes brimming. "I know there are no more planes to California tonight, but I will just sit and wait there until tomorrow morning and then Mommy will meet me at the Los Angeles airport. I just miss everybody too much."

"You'll be so much more comfortable here in the bed at Grandma's house instead of sitting up in a chair at the airport all night, Alexander. Let's call Mommy and see what she says."

Mommy assured him he could come home tomorrow if he still wanted to do so, but he needed to sleep in bed that night. Surrounded with photos of the loved ones back home while listening to a lullaby tape—one he had used in babyhood—he finally managed to fall asleep. The next morning the world looked a little brighter, and he stayed the full ten days with no more crashes.

Arriving this year, he quickly assured Grandpa and me he would not have a meltdown this time. His only stipulation was that he be allowed to sleep in the back guest bedroom, which had no strange photos of his ancestors hanging on the walls, as did the other guest room. This was an easy choice for us, because we remembered his having been spooked by the family artifacts when he was assigned to that room the first year he had visited. In fact, he had spent most of the first night in there systematically removing the photos and other memorabilia from their places of display and putting them in the hallway.

At 2:00 a.m. I had been awakened by a strange thumping, and upon exiting my bedroom, I encountered lying in the hall "the headless woman" he had placed there. I chuckled when I contrasted my experience of having lovingly assembled and displayed the dressmaker's form clothed in my grandmother's wedding dress with his experience of being frightened by a decapitated human-like creature lurking at the foot of his bed. As a child, I had spent many a night at my own grandparents' home awake until the early hours of daylight when the strange, shadowy nocturnal invaders in their house could be banished in the sunshine. In retrospect I wish I had had in my childhood Alexander's confidence to get out of bed and deal with the enemy instead of lying there paralyzed.

So as we sat on the swing in the late afternoon shadows, enjoying our tea and graham crackers, and welcoming the slight cooling in the air after another hot, humid Tennessee summer day, I was puzzled by Alexander's question.

"Why do you want to hit my knee with your hand?" I asked.

"Well, Grandma, you keep telling people you have metal knees and I was wondering if they feel different than regular knees."

The subject of my knee replacements had come up several times during this visit, like when we passed through security at the airport and I had to get scanned and patted down. We had also talked about my knees while discussing the kinds of surgery he and other folks have had.

"I was born with a broken heart, and I had to have it fixed when I was two years old," Alexander had explained to someone at the swimming pool, when asked about the looping scar under his left shoulder blade, now faded after five years. The whole family had been so relieved when the defect in his heart had been repaired in routine modern-day surgery. I am old enough to remember when the very first of these surgeries was being done, and they were anything but routine back then.

"Sure, you can hit my knee with your hand, as long as you do it gently enough so that neither of us gets hurt."

Winding up ever so slightly, as he had watched a baseball pitcher do on the mound at the ball game we attended a few days earlier, his seven-year-old hand firmly struck the newest of my metal knees, just above the kneecap. It was a soft blow, and no one got hurt by it.

"Yep, it feels like metal, all right," he declared, grinning. He leaned forward and dipped his Honey Maid into the cup of tea he had been sipping. I freshened my cup and decided to dip my Honey Maid, too.

I wish I had thought to ask him if I could put my hand over his mended heart. I would have liked to have discovered if the beating of a heart which is no longer broken feels different from the way any other heart feels.

ANGELA BRITNELL

Sarah's Choice

"**D**isgraceful. Young people these days can't keep their hands off each other in public. Can you imagine what Father would have said if we'd behaved that way?"

Margaret's face wrinkled in disgust at the sight of a couple kissing passionately on the station platform, completely oblivious to anything going on around them. She pointedly smoothed down her brown tweed skirt, placed her gold-rimmed half-glasses more firmly on her nose, and went back to reading her book, not waiting for an answer.

Sarah suppressed a smile. Margaret had been a prissy girl, never any fun as a sister, and sixty years hadn't changed her one bit. But the smile faded as she remembered the suitcase in the luggage compartment behind them, and the trunk packed and stored at her neighbor's house ready to be sent on when she was settled.

Settled. With Margaret. In Margaret's house. A shiver ran through Sarah's stomach until she thought she might be sick.

Her eyes were inexorably drawn back to the young couple. The man flung off his heavy backpack and wrapped his arms around the girl, lifting her off her feet to swing her around, joyfully kissing her the whole time. The girl shone with love as she wound her arms around his neck. He put her gently back down, cradled her face in his hands, and kissed her again as though he never wanted to let go.

William. Forty years ago her father ran him off saying he wasn't good enough. But Sarah hadn't forgotten his kiss. The one nobody knew about. The one they'd sneaked that evening by the back door after her father ordered him to leave. William's intense blue eyes had stared at her, fixing her in his memory. Sarah knew that was what he'd done, because it was what she'd been doing—imprinting every taste and sensation on her heart, while knowing it was going to have to last a lifetime.

Instinctively, her hand planted on the window to get closer. The young man pushed away slightly to rake the girl from head to toe with his eyes, her response an exuberant swirl of her hips, setting the short, red dress in motion so it moved in waves around her long, slim legs.

Sarah turned away. It was too much. She felt like a voyeur, although the couple plainly didn't care. Why should they?

"You've gone very red in the face, Sarah. I hope you've been taking your blood pressure medicine. It'll be very inconvenient if you get ill on the train."

Margaret wasn't worried, only cross. What a surprise.

"I'm fine. It's just a little warm in here." Sarah fanned her hot cheeks with a magazine as the train pulled away from the station. Over the paper she sneaked one last glance at the lovers and watched them walk away, their steps matching.

"I hope you're not going to be fussy. Your room gets the afternoon sun, and I don't want to hear non-stop complaints about how hot it is."

Sarah checked the urge to be rude. She couldn't afford to annoy Margaret. Father's recent death had left her homeless and penniless, the insurance policies secretly cashed-in long ago, and the house sold immediately to pay gambling debts nobody had known about. It had horrified Margaret. A lack of self-discipline always disgusted her whether regarding food, sex, or money. Sarah had taken it as stolidly as she'd taken everything else in life—there'd been no alternative, as far as she could see.

And now this, the inevitable sharing of her life again with Margaret. Yet again there was no other choice. Her options had seemingly gone long ago when Father declared she would stay home to take care of him after their mother's early death. Margaret, the oldest and cleverest, was allowed to go to university, train as a teacher, and work. Both girls were strictly discouraged from mixing with men. Sarah was certain Margaret had always been obedient on that score.

Sarah suspected most of her acquaintances considered her old and would be surprised to find out she'd only just turned sixty. That wasn't old these days. Goodness, you read of people doing all kinds of things at that age.

She could take off and travel the world, bungee jump from a bridge in the rain forest, swim with the dolphins in Florida, or ride a motorbike across the Sahara. But who was she fooling? She didn't like heights, couldn't swim, and didn't have a driver's license. A voice nagged in her head and asked, Why not? Her answer was a sad one. Because other people had told her she couldn't, and she'd accepted it.

Obedience had led to this. Dull gray hair, boring clothes, and the prospect of spending the rest of her life in her dreary sister's quiet bungalow in Devon, with meals prescribed for every day of the week and a constitutional walk along the sea front every day for their health. God, it sounded exactly like Jane Austen describing the life of a downtrodden poor relation.

Sarah opened her handbag, watching Margaret from the corner of her eye, and took out the piece of paper. It was amazing what computers could help you find out. If she hadn't got to talking to the girl at the library one day, it wouldn't have occurred to her. Alison had chattered on about looking up an old school friend on the Internet, and before she could decide if it was wise or not, Sarah had mentioned William. A few clicks on the keyboard, and it'd been right in front of her. His name, address, and telephone number. Alison had laughed and asked if Sarah was going to call him. Sarah had given a tight little smile and answered, "Maybe."

No doubt William was married with children and grandchildren. His handsome features must have blurred, and his thick ebony hair was either all gone or turned thin and gray. His eyes would be hidden behind bifocal glasses, and the bright sea-blue dulled to ordinary cloudy-day boring. William's tall, muscular body would have the beginnings of a stoop and touches of arthritis, and his stomach would roll over the top of his trouser waist.

That unappealing picture was the only way to stop from doing something silly. Sarah had to convince herself he'd be as ordinary as any other sixty-five-year-old man. Then she must look again in the mirror and see what time had done to her, too. The combination of those two things should do the trick.

When the young couple so obviously in love today look at each other in forty years, what would they see? The truth of wrinkles and baldness, or the glowing skin and strong bodies of their youth? If it was true love, they would look past the obvious, see into each other's heart, and the rest would blur into insignificance.

Sarah smiled very discreetly, folded the paper carefully, and put it away in her purse. She'd been obedient too long. The only thing she planned to obey from now on was her heart, letting it take her where it chose.

Maybe it would be life at Margaret's, but maybe, just maybe, it wouldn't.

S. R. LEE

Consignment Store

"Such a lot of cute little frames!" I say to new customers. "Those two at the end are sterling silver. You can see the mark on the back."

I don't mention that this new generation just uses those Lucite frames you can buy anywhere, but the old folks really like to have their true silver frames.

"We have a good collection of vases, too," I'll add, waving toward the shelf where fancy bud vases sit in front of plainer ones. You'd think people would have more care for their old folks than to bring flowers in plain florist vases. Don't families care how the things in their old folks' rooms look? But of course, I wouldn't say that to my customers.

This shop, Miss Nancy's Gifts, is definitely more genteel than the pawnshop business. Just imagine taking in used things, having to hold them a certain time, and then giving them back if the owner brings in the money. I have a simple gift shop which I run all by myself, though my real name isn't Nancy. My illiterate mother named me Rita Maydene Lockhart—no name for a businesswoman of genteel ways. I use Nancy M. Chase as my business name, and I pay my rent on time.

Well, I did until now. Good thing it's the end of the month. In two more days, I would have written another rent check. Now I need that money. I know how to play the game. I like the game I've kept going in the shop for eight years now, but the kind that involves escape and reestablishment is more than I really want to fool with.

In the game I play, I take in a new consignment and sell the good pieces the next day. If a piece seems unique, I'll hold it a while, maybe even six or eight months. Often I need to clean things up. With the clothes, I check for name tags and laundry marks. For frames, I have to remove the pictures. Really old pictures can be a problem to take out when they've been in silver frames for fifty years, or maybe seventy or eighty, for all I know. The edges stick, so I have to scrape them off without leaving scratches. Good thing I don't want the picture. In fact, I'm always careful to cut it up and get it out to the trash right away. No telling who's going to be browsing through the shop. I polish up the frames, too, so they look quite fresh, not like they did sitting in the nursing-home room with the old folks. I've never been accused of having any family piece, although occasionally some woman will be really pleased to find one.

"Look at this frame! It's so much like the one with my grandmother's picture."

Often, she buys it, pleased to have something similar to a family heirloom. She thinks she'll have a pair of them, except I know she won't. Sometimes her family resemblance is so strong to the picture I have just torn up, I worry a little. If my hands shake, I hide them under the counter and breathe slowly.

The ladies browsing like for me not to bother them or try to sell them anything.

Now, a man, he usually wants me to help him. He feels odd in a gift shop anyway.

"Can I help you, sir? . . . For your daughter's birthday? How old is she? . . . In college? Why, right over here are some lovely earrings, or perhaps she'd like an old-fashioned brooch. College girls are old enough to appreciate quality and grace. I know a father likes to give his girls nice things."

By then he's relieved to have someone who understands his difficult decision.

We do have some really nice silver and pearl pins sometimes

or some old-fashioned coral. I never keep any diamonds. This is a gift shop, not a jewelry store. I have a contact who arranges a fair price for me through a jeweler in Michigan, far enough away that the diamond is not likely to be traced. About every third time, I can tell a supplier who brought in a diamond that it was not real and the ring or brooch is only worth thirty or forty dollars. I make a nice profit that way—my fifty percent commission of the thirty dollars plus the difference between what I say I got for it and what I really got. This shop is not a hobby with me. Business is business, and I give a fair return to my suppliers. After all, they take the things for free.

But the truth is, they also bring in a lot of junk. Good-hearted people take a lot of nonsense to nursing homes—bright-red little stuffed Santas at Christmas and pink ceramic hearts at Valentine's. In a way, they know nursing homes are good places to "lose" things, so they bring jolly junk. I give a set price for it, maybe a quarter. Then I put it in a box in the second-hand clothes store I run catty-cornered down the alley. There my customers are quite a different sort. While the mothers are looking through the clothes, their children find the box. Everything for a dollar.

Some of my suppliers are very clever with clothes. They watch how the "resident" weakens and starts to wear only washable clothes, easy to put on. That old woman might have four woolen suits hanging in her closet. Slip one out in June, and no one will notice. It won't be missed until November, and by then maybe the old woman will be dead, or just lying in that bed.

I tell my people, "Go ahead if you need to and trip up the old biddy before the weather gets cold and she starts thinking about her warm clothes. With a broken hip, she won't be walking over to that closet to find anything."

Some of my people have been with me a long time. They know I can give a nice little addition in cash to that minimum wage the nursing home pays for doing all the dirty work.

The night shift is best for a supplier. Not many people are about, and usually the supplier knows where they are. It's not hard to slip quietly along in those rubber-soled shoes nurses wear. Should a supervisor challenge her, she can say she was checking Mrs. So and So's diaper because she seemed to be getting a rash.

If the old people wake and see my supplier going through a drawer or walking toward the door with a favorite keepsake in her hand, no one will believe them the next morning. Sometimes a supplier is sly enough to rearrange things so the pictures or vases are in different positions. After a while the old person will be confused about what is where, and a skilled supplier can lift out a good deal of it.

One of my men has perfected the art of nighttime theft. He sits down with the wakeful old people and talks friendly and soft until they fall asleep. He becomes their trusted friend who will gladly look in the drawer for a favorite letter and read it to them, no matter how many times. After all, the drawer with the loved letters also holds other precious things: rings, bank statements, cash. The old people never think my man is the guilty one. No, he is the friend who comforts them in the night.

There's little worry. Nurses and family will decide the old woman is getting dotty should she say that someone goes through her things at night. Should she say, "The staff has a gift shop where they sell our things," everyone will think she is just hallucinating. Supervisors rarely stay long enough to see a pattern of theft.

What nonsense! Of course the staff doesn't have a gift shop. I do. I take things on consignment. I pay the rent here, and I earn the profits for my work. I run most of the risk. A supplier doesn't have to tell me his name if he accepts my offering price. It may be low, but it's pure profit for him. I like that arrangement because then my profit margin is high. But the way to get really good pieces and keep this shop known for the occasional bargain antique among the "gifts" is to pay a fair consignment price to regular suppliers. They get a higher percentage, but I get better-quality things.

I keep the regulars' names and phone numbers, along with a numbered code of what they brought, in a shoebox in the back of a closet. Of course, I'm a modern shopkeeper with a computer cash register and records and tax returns on another computer in the back storeroom. If police ever investigate, they'll find plenty on the computers, a little muddled perhaps, but I'll say I am a middle-aged person, not entirely computer literate. Actually, I enjoy fabricating my records—what came in and how much I paid for it, when it went out and what I got. Naturally, I do a lot of business in cash. Nowadays, I accept credit cards, but I don't use one myself. Why leave a paper trail?

The greatest danger to my business is having my regulars know my name. If one of them is ever arrested, she might betray me. Or maybe one would find Jesus and decide to confess her sins and go the straight and narrow. I try to watch for the signs of religion and give good prices to counteract it. Minimum wage doesn't encourage the straight and narrow.

Another problem is that my good suppliers can clean out a small nursing home or one floor of a large one in about six months. I encourage my best people to change jobs every now and then. Those large nursing homes might get suspicious if someone were to ask for a transfer to a different floor. On the other hand, those big institutions are so impersonal that the staff doesn't even know each other. The residents are so grateful for any friendliness, that a skilled supplier can find out what's valuable in just a few days of kindly chat.

Even a medium-sized city can sustain a shop like mine if the shopkeeper works out a good line of suppliers. I thought I'd be set for life if I would just be mildly charming to the customers and extra cautious with the suppliers and accounting.

Now I have to be gone before daybreak. Lucky I'm by myself. I can pack every inch of the car, the best jewelry under the seats and the other stuff in the trunk. I wouldn't want to rent a trailer. It might be traceable.

Imagine one of my suppliers wanting to be a detective! I thought *I* was the devious person in this scheme. She's not even honest. I'll bet she's going to keep that one-hundred percent profit she's made from me for the past six months. Okay, so she outsmarted me. The problem is that tricking me was her goal. She had patience, too, bringing in just one or two pieces every month and telling me stories, as though she were experienced at nursing-home work. What's with this woman? Who would do that if she didn't really need to?

She certainly looked the part. She came in here with those white shoes nurses wear. Her hair hung down sort of bedraggled like tacky people's hair these days, and she had on an old green sweater most nights.

And then, to beat all, she warned me. She came in here a week ago last Thursday with two straw purses, a big plain one and a little coin purse with a decoration in the shape of Xs across it in pink raffia, and she also brought a little silver fairy with wings made of gold wire. It was pretty and not like anything I'd ever had in the store. I thought it too valuable and considered refusing the piece. Any friend or relative who had ever visited that person in the nursing home would recognize it in a flash.

"The plain purse, I'll put out tomorrow, and the other, maybe in a month or so, but I don't know about this fairy, Shug," I said. "It's so different. I'll have to hold it a long time. Might be recognized."

"Well, I need a good commission on it. I can't wait too long."

She'd never put this kind of pressure on me, but lots of them do, so I didn't think much about it. She'd never even told me her

CONSIGNMENT STORE

name or talked about her personal situation the way many suppliers do, trying to jack up their commission by seeming needy. What a fool I was! Instead of being suspicious that she wasn't one to play on my sympathies, I had simply enjoyed being free from the pressure.

Anyway, this was the first time I'd ever said I'd have to delay on payment. She wasn't pleased.

I said, "But you can see it's too valuable to put out until that old woman dies or you change jobs for a while. I'll be able to price that at a hundred dollars. You'll get thirty-five pure profit, but you'll have to wait."

"Well, maybe I should just take it back. They won't have missed it yet."

No one had ever suggested taking anything back. That should have bothered me more.

We sat for a while.

"Maybe you could put it out in just a couple of weeks."

"Way too soon. This is a hold-for-a-year piece."

I turned it in my hands. The little statue was slightly tarnished. It would need cleaning up. I knew I wouldn't be putting it out for months.

"I might use it for the Christmas season."

"That's still eight months away. I'll just take it back."

She reached out with the piece of tissue paper she'd brought it in and wrapped it up again.

I was miffed. "Well, forty dollars, then."

"Can you give me the money now?"

"You know that's not how this business runs. You get your money when I get mine." I tried to sound outraged.

She stood up, shrugged herself into the old sweater. "Well, I'll think about it. I'm not taking it back right away."

The next afternoon I met my trouble in the form of ladies. Three of them entered the shop—casual spring clothes, nice

205

purses. I recognize upper crust. One had her hair tucked under a straw hat with a wide brim and really snappy straw sandals. A little early in the spring for those, I thought. She stayed near the door, looking closely at some baskets, so I didn't see her face very well. I thought about showing her some little pictures made from straw, but then I noticed that her hat and sandals were decorated with pink raffia in the form of Xs. Some odd feeling prickled the back of my neck, so I left her alone to look at the baskets. The second lady went from spot to spot, picking up bud vases with what seemed like real interest. I would have given her my favorite line—"Such a lot of cute little vases!"—but the third was distracting me, looking quickly but closely at every shelf without touching a thing. She came to my desk.

"I'm searching for a special piece, and I hear you sometimes have unusual things," she said. "My great aunt in Bellevue Nursing Home had a little silver angel with gold wire wings. It was very dear to her, and now it's disappeared. Have you seen anything like that?"

I think of myself as a fairly good actress under stress, but her question was a considerable shock. I had to put my hands down on the edge of my desk to keep them still, while I stretched my lips into a smile.

"Why, no, I don't think I have. We have mostly ceramic things, not much silver."

Any glance around the shop would tell her that "mostly ceramic" was a joke. What with the pillows, baskets, candles, and artificial flowers, to say nothing of the book and CD section, which included a boombox or two, this shop was definitely a potpourri of things, though I did try to feature the nicer vases and frames.

She gave a slow look around the whole shop.

"Could I leave my name and ask you to call me if you see such an angel? I have a card."

She held out a little white business card with elegant lettering.

CONSIGNMENT STORE

"Why, yes, of course." I didn't want it, but I put the card in my desk drawer.

"Wait." She held out her hand. "I'll write what I want. Otherwise, I'm afraid you'll forget."

She didn't sound rude, just practical, and I didn't take offense. I handed back her card, she wrote a few words, and I put it back into my desk drawer.

She turned casually. "Well, girls, time to go." Without hesitation, both of the others started for the door. I watched them moving out so promptly without a last glance at any of my goods. Something was wrong. The one in the straw hat held the door for the others, then turned and looked me in the face. I had seen her before. Where? Who? As she went out the door, she dropped something white into a basket.

Once their car drove away, I looked. It was an envelope. Inside was a folded paper which said, "Read the small print."

I took out the card. Underneath the lady's name, which was in a beautiful curly font, was a line of simple, small capital letters. THE THREE GRACES DETECTIVE AGENCY.

The phone rang, but I did not answer. When the message machine came on, I heard a voice say, "Is she really that rattled?" Then Shug's voice came straight and strong. "Your fingerprints dusted out really well off the fairy. Because the police don't like to be bothered after regular hours, we won't go by the station until tomorrow morning."

So that was Shug under the straw hat, not a tired worker at all, but a mean rich woman who wants to play detective.

I can get away, and believe me, I will. I'm much too nice a lady to spend time behind bars. Here I thought I was doing the underpaid a favor by augmenting their income, and someone almost turns me in just for the fun of the puzzle.

I don't like this puzzle. Tonight I'll have to get far away and lay low. I must find a fence for my best pieces if I'm going to finance a hideout.

But I'll leave these traitors a diversion. The file with the real names and coded records will be sitting on the counter in plain sight, as if I forgot it. Tracing those folks should busy police detectives for a while.

The old folks will miss their friendly attendants.

OLIVE MAYGER

The Unriddler

She smiled brightly. "It's a breakthrough!"

He'd never seen her so perky. He gave the customary "continue" wave. It was a nice October afternoon. He liked the way the sun came through the window by his chair.

"It dawned on me just yesterday when we were raking the yard. It's a big one. We always seem to be raking something."

She looked at him for confirmation.

Another wave.

"Yes. That's where it came from." She was emphatic, balanced on the edge of the tall oak stool she preferred, heels hooked over the middle rung, hands clutched together. "And, we've caught it!"

He raised his eyebrows. "Caught it?"

"From the maples."

"The maples," he reflected.

She nodded energetically and went on. "For years and years we've raked and piled and bagged and mulched all those leaves." She looked away. "All those leaves," she whispered. Then she was back. "We've embraced them. Got them down our shirts and jeans. Tracked them into the house. Ground them into the carpet." She was gaining momentum. "Inhaled them! Digested them! Heavens, we've flushed them! And now," she lowered her voice for emphasis, "we've caught it."

"And that is…?" he asked paternally.

"Deciduousness."

He peered at her.

"That's why our house is a mess! That's why there are crumbs on the couch. That's why there are papers all over. That's why our clothes are on the floor. *Things fall off us! Like the leaves fall off the trees!* We can't help it!"

She was jubilant.

Unwelcome suspicion edged into his mind. The room seemed to fade into premature November gray. His back hurt.

She stretched her arms above her, sighed deeply, relaxed into a contented hoop, and rocked gently on her perch.

"To think I feared we were suffocating from some kind of, of—well, eccentric messiness. That I was a poor housekeeper, of all things." She gave a "silly me" smirk. "And all these years, we've been unsuspecting victims of an obviously unusual but naturally imposed malady." She shone with certainty. "I've looked it up, but it's not in the medical journals yet. They're obviously waiting for the seasons to change before they release their findings so folks won't become alarmed. Just think. There may not be a cure. But not to worry!" Her full cheerfulness returned. "At *our* house we're fortunate. We're already used to it. We're a verifiable statistic."

She straightened, stretched again, slid off the stool, and extended her hand.

He stood slowly. For some reason he remembered he hadn't gotten his flu shot yet.

"Thank you, doctor," she said. It was obvious she was deeply grateful. "You have no idea what a difference coming here has made."

It was a hearty handshake on her part. She put her hand over his in a final gesture of genuine thanks. Bits of dry grass and tiny seeds fell from her jacket sleeve.

She stopped at the doorway to rummage through her bag for her keys. A golf ball surfaced and fell out.

It bounced away unheeded as she waved goodbye.

LOUISE COLLN

Long Shadows

"There's a place I want to show you before we check out the cave," he announced, pulling the truck over to the side of the primitive road. "It's just a short walk from here."

Kayce followed him across the wet ground. She soon realized that a short walk for Sam was a ten-mile trek to her. She knew he kept their pace slow for her sake. Still, the cold mountain air and slight upward climb caused her breathing to become stressed long before she was willing to let him be aware of it. She was glad when they came out onto a level space. Then she held her breath altogether in wonder.

They were deep in pines left untouched for years. The discarded needles piled underfoot gave her an uncanny feeling of walking on something less stable than earth. The trees seemed to drink in all semblance of sound, so that the sibilance of wind through the boughs and the peevish call of a distant crow were only different incarnations of silence.

"Oh, beautiful," Kayce breathed in a spontaneous cry of delight, held in total absorption by her surroundings. She forgot even Sam's presence until he made a movement. As she turned toward him, she was surprised by his intense gaze on her. There was a look in his eyes that she couldn't, or chose not to, name.

"I knew you would be able to appreciate it as it should be appreciated," he said. "I come here sometimes, just to soak in it. This is the first time I've brought anyone with me."

Kayce was silent.

"Aren't you going to ask me what it is?"

She looked around. "It's a forest," she said simply. "Does it have to be anything more?"

"It's a tiny ghost town, Kayce. See the traces of two old trails crossing there beside those four trees? Men came to the Smokies in the 1850s thinking they'd find gold or silver. They left some places behind. Like this one. They mostly lived in tents, but there's logs scattered around and some pits over there in the rocks where they dug. They had no idea where the gold would have been if there had been gold. And there may have been some. Come on."

He caught her hand and Kayce felt surprisingly welcome warmth. Could she really feel warmth through their gloves? She wished they weren't wearing gloves as they walked together through the trees.

"But where was the gold?"

"There's a story that one man found gold but never told anyone where, and it may be just a story. There was a little gold around, but the rush didn't last long and this really isn't big enough to be called a ghost town like the ones in the West."

"Okay. We'll call it a ghost village."

He looked at her and grinned. "Or even a ghost wide place in the road."

She felt something more substantial than the shifting needles under her foot. "Wait. There's something."

She drew her hand from his and pried a piece of tin from the dirt. "Look, Sam, it's an old tin can."

He brushed some of the dirt off the can as she held it. "Smashed up pretty good and used as a target by the looks of it. See, there's at least five bullet holes in it."

Kayce giggled. "Oh, those were from the shootout." She held the can up, trying to see through the holes, and then dropped it.

"The shootout?" There was at the same time a smile and a frown on his face.

"The one between Black Bart and Sweet Simon."

"In the street, of course."

She enjoyed hearing him move into her world. "Where they cross."

"At high noon."

"Probably. It was hard to tell with all the trees, and the old gentleman's watch was broken."

"The old gentleman?"

"Jonathon. Jonathon Gold. Father of the beautiful Lotta."

"Over whom the shootout was shot out?"

"And for whom the town was named. Jonathon really meant to start a college town, not a gold-rush town at all. And he thought it would be nice to name it after his daughter."

"Lotta Gold."

"Right. He was sorry he'd done that when the rough element came in with their picks and shovels and all that."

"Not what you'd consider desirable elements in a college town."

"Not a professor in the bunch. Well, one man who'd got into gold-rushing after he was kicked out of the chemistry department of Harvard."

"You're going to tell me why?"

"How do I know why? I haven't read the personnel files of Harvard." She hesitated. "It might have something to do with his nickname, though. Black Bart."

"Maybe there was an explosion."

"Maybe. Black Bart lived dangerously."

"And wore guns slung low on his hips."

"Right under his pickax. Anyway, after they all dug around and didn't find any gold, they saw Lotta. Both Black Bart and Sweet Simon fell in love with her." Since Kayce had been the one to drop his hand, she decided she should be the one to bring them together again. She reached to grasp his hand, palm to palm.

"Of course, she loved Sweet Simon." Without missing a beat of the story, he removed his hand to take his glove off. He pulled hers off and dropped them beside the tin can, then closed their bare hands together. Kayce felt a stirring inside herself as deep as if it were bodies pressing together.

"No, actually, she loved Black Bart, scarred as he was. She thought she could reform him. But the old gentleman favored Sweet Simon." She struggled to stay in the lighthearted tenor of the story, to keep her emotions from showing in her voice.

His own deepened voice told her that she hadn't succeeded, as he picked up the story. "So they decided to shoot it out."

She watched him slide her other glove off and drop it at their feet. She slipped her hand inside his large welcoming glove before she spoke. The back of her hand curled against his palm inside the glove.

"Sweet Simon challenged Black Bart, and he couldn't say no. It wasn't done then. But Lotta knew the truth. Black Bart, having been raised to be a professor, couldn't shoot for shucks. He had a bad habit of pulling out his pickax instead of his gun. Had to hit a bear over the head pretty hard once when he did that back in the forest. So she hatched a plan."

"I can't wait to hear it."

For a minute she only heard his faint accent on the words, "I can't wait."

Everything inside her wanted to keep the moment going. "It was pretty simple. She just told Sweet Simon that the gold was way out in Colorado and such places. He left at midnight."

"That's the end of the story? That doesn't explain the holes." He gestured toward the can with their entwined hands.

"Of course it explains the holes. After Black Bart had spent so many hours practicing, he had to shoot something just to show her how good he was. So she hung the can from a tree limb, and every morning he shot at it from their tent. Hit it several times, too. You can see."

"And she did succeed in reforming him."

"Immediately. They lived happily ever after, riding off into sunsets."

She turned to face him, their arms folding like wind-up toys to pull their bodies close. As her hands moved inside his, she was intensely aware of the fiery feel of his toughened palm against her softer skin.

He leaned toward her.

JAMES A. CRUTCHFIELD

The Wild Horses of the Pryor Mountains

Ask folks who live along the sparsely populated Montana-Wyoming border about the origin of the wild horses that roam the surrounding Pryor Mountains and most will tell you that the herds sprang from domesticated stock that had been released over the years. While there can be no doubt that onetime ranch horses have contributed their part to the propagation of the hundreds of wild horses that graze the parched landscape of the Pryors, the line of Montana mustangs actually dates back all the way to the original herds of livestock brought to Mexico by Spanish conquistadors in 1519.

When the United States Bureau of Land Management announced in 1964 that two hundred wild horses living in the Pryor Mountains would be rounded up and sold at auction, concerned landowners, who had always looked upon the herds as part of their heritage, sued to protect the animals. Five years later, several thousand acres of the region containing the horses were declared the Pryor Mountain National Wild Horse Range and placed under the administration of the federal government.

To visit the refuge is an experience one will never forget. As the region is approached from the Montana side, a visible difference in the terrain becomes clear. Traveling south, the lush Montana prairie rapidly surrenders to a dry, stark landscape of jagged tableland populated by meager grasses. Here and there are recognizable tepee rings—circles of field stones used by Indian families hundreds of years ago to anchor the edges of their buffalo-skin lodges. The ground is rocky and dry, and hot winds drive small clouds of dust from the impoverished soil.

The wait won't be long until the first horses make their appearance. They are wild and free and totally unafraid, sometimes straying right down onto the hardtop highway. But hiking a short distance from the little-traveled road, say a mile or two, provides the best viewing opportunity. If the weather is hot, and it always is in the summer, you can scan the horizon and pick out individuals or small groups gathered among clumps of trees that provide cooling shade for the horses. They will rest there, standing for hours at a time, until dusk draws near.

The herds are usually small, consisting of a stallion and perhaps three or four mares and as many foals. Not long ago, on a scorching July day, I confronted a herd about this size, and as one of our group dropped down into a coulee, hoping to drive the animals toward the rest of us for a better view, the buckskin stallion spotted him. Nervously rounding up his small family, the lean horse nudged his brood across the grassland. Somewhere along the way, one of the mares and two colts separated from the others, and the stallion became frantic. After assuring himself that the remaining mare and her offspring were safe, he launched a search for his other mate.

It was a sight to behold. The mighty buckskin ran effortlessly, gliding through the brush and grass stubble, down into a coulee, up again, head held high, ever searching for his lost family. Spying his missing kin in the distance, he was gone in a flash, speeding across the prairie to reunite his harem.

SUZANNE BRUNSON

Minnie Pearl, Price Tags, and Typewriters

"How-dee! I'm just so proud to be here!"

It was Minnie Pearl's raucous greeting as she strode onto the Ryman Auditorium stage Saturday nights as part of the Grand Ole Opry cast. It was her loud and folksy claim to fame because it meant she was ready with her tomfoolery and country humor that wasn't always so country, but always funny.

I was excited. I had an interview with Minnie Pearl at her yellow gingerbread museum down near Music Row in Nashville. I was editor of the *Senior Sentinel* at that time, a newspaper for Nashville "seniors." I looked forward to doing the story because Minnie was the best interview in Music City. I had no doubt it would be fun.

On stage Minnie wore a fancied-up version of a housedress with a full ruffled skirt falling just below her knees and featuring even more ruffles around both the neckline and puffy short sleeves. She wore tights with her black Mary Janes, and her signature flat straw hat with a wide brim set atop her upswept hair. Flowers encircled the hat band, and, of course, there was her "forgotten" price tag dangling just far enough to the right so that she supposedly couldn't see her faux pas. Her inference was that only a country bumpkin from Grinder's Switch would forget to take off the tag.

Many people believed she always marked the price at $1.98, but she gave me a real scoop.

"I have run up on some that had other prices," she said and winked. "Like a $1.95, and I even found $2.69 on one."

Minnie held a special place in the hearts of country music fans. She was classy gone country, and the fans loved it. She did "I'm from the sticks" better than any comedian before or since. Her sharp ear for the nuanced language of the rural South, combined with the tutelage of some of the best in the business, put her on the top of the heap. Minnie never looked down her elegant patrician nose at anyone.

Minnie's museum was quaint and, if anything, the best representation of any country music star. The highlight was a giant straw hat strung from the ceiling, the obligatory dangling price tag waving like a streamer blowing from a whirling fan. The famous straw hat was created from plastic garbage bags, and one of the flowers was a painted Bundt pan. The giant hat was a very good likeness of those Minnie bought from a Lawrence County Amish woman who weaved all of her hats and also made miniatures for the museum gift shop.

The museum featured several handcrafted dioramas depicting highlights of Minnie's life, from growing up as Sarah Ophelia Colley in her hometown of Centerville, Tennessee, to the Grand Ole Opry. It also featured a limited edition Minnie Pearl doll. Buy one and she'd autograph it in a place that would make you blush. I still regret not buying a doll, or at least a miniature hat, but I had a deadline to meet.

The interview went well, and that night after supper, while sitting at the kitchen table, I started pecking out the story on my electric typewriter. I'd grown up on a manual, so when my husband gave me the electric from his office, I felt pretty uptown. Minnie was getting a very positive write-up for the *Senior Sentinel*. Peck. Peck. Peck. The electric took a soft, light touch, but Minnie deserved a story pounded out on an old manual typewriter, and I pictured myself bent over an antique black Underwood like I remembered from my days as a cub reporter.

I had spent most of my childhood in Georgia, hearing that my dad was a "ramblin' wreck from Georgia Tech and a hell of an engineer." I went to "that journalism school at the agricultural college over in Athens." Then I married a Tennessean and relocated to Rocky Top country and the world of Tennessee hillbillies. My hillbilly had attended Vanderbilt, and I got my engagement ring one beautiful spring day on a bench outside the old engineering building. I was persuaded to leave the Peach State.

The clincher to keeping me in Nashville and happy was learning that my idol in the newspaper business, the late editor of the Atlanta *Constitution*, Ralph McGill, had felt he could get a pretty good education in the Volunteer State.

I met Mr. McGill once, if only briefly for a handshake. My sister had called the paper and asked to do interviews for our high school newspaper. He agreed, and my sister let me—the embarrassment of her life—tag along, more than likely coerced by our mother. While my sister interviewed the premier newsman of the South, I sat in a huge rocking chair in Celestine Sibley's office.

Ms. Sibley was another renowned columnist and reporter and shared an office with Harold Martin, in the same league. I was a young fourteen, so I just sat with my legs dangling and rocked while they asked me all about my school and the newspaper and did I like to write and I said yes. I'd even sent in a piece to my hometown weekly about how I'd "traveled down to Albany, Georgia, to spend a week during summer vacation with former Smyrna resident, Miss Lynn Smith."

I figured Celestine and Harold were probably pretty impressed with my talent showing up at such a young age.

"Miss Sibley, that is a really big typewriter," I said, pointing at the big brown machine. "My mom has a black one at home, but it's not nearly as big as yours. She took it off to Florida State her freshman year of college."

"Does she like to write?"

"Oh, not really, just letters to my grandparents, stuff like that, but she reads all the time and could probably type on your typewriter since she is church organist and her hands are pretty nimble. Anyway, her typewriter is all in a million pieces now because my father tinkered with it and couldn't put it back together. It's sitting on a big old oak desk down in the basement right now."

"What does he do?"

"My father? Oh, he's an engineer at Lockheed."

"Well, that's what engineers do—take things apart."

"Yes, ma'am, you're right. But I don't think my mother was giving much consideration to his career choice when she saw what he'd done."

Ms. Sibley's fingers began tapping away at her keys, and she was smiling. I looked over at Mr. Martin, who was leaning way back in his squeaky chair, and he was smiling, too, while he flipped a yellow pencil between his thumb and index finger. He had on a white shirt with his sleeves rolled up. I noticed that because my dad always wore short-sleeved shirts so he wouldn't ruin his cuffs rubbing them all over a drafting table, or while dismantling things.

"Oh, ma'am, are you typing anything I just said?"

"Well, yes, hon, it's a cute story."

"Oh, please don't print that! My parents will kill me."

"No? Are you sure?"

"Yes, ma'am, that would be off the record."

There. I'd used my first official interview tool and gotten myself out of a little potential trouble.

Years later, after the infamous electric had been packed away, replaced with great temerity by a computer, I found myself antiquing with my in-laws in Denham Springs, Louisiana. Antiques put this little town on the map, and we were anxious to hit every shop. My sister-in-law and I wandered off on our own.

We picked our first store at the corner of the first block, planning to go up one side of the street and then back down the other side. We took two steps in the door, and there it was. An Underwood. A little rough around the edges, but all in one piece and still able to accept a writer's pounding. I was jubilant and bought it on the spot, forgetting to barter or finagle. I would not make a good horse trader.

My sister-in-law and I then lugged the Underwood to the trunk of my brother-in-law's car. It was not so much a trunk as a rear crevice in some type of hatchback. That was one heavy typewriter, and I'd put it up against any desktop computer.

We entered our second antique store and my mother-in-law called out, motioning for me from behind a wall of merchandise. There, on a shelf located in the back of the store, hidden behind a makeshift shelf pushed tight against an iron water pipe, sat a black manual typewriter.

"It's a Royal," she said.

"Oh, you've got a bargain there," the owner said.

The store owner assured me the typewriter had been owned, cared for, and loved by a local writer who was finally ready to part with it. I bought it. After years of being captivated by and searching for old black manuals, I had found two in one day.

With that typewriter shoved into the other side of the crevice in my brother-in-law's hatchback, I took a step back, folded my arms across my chest, and smiled. We did a little more shopping, but the oak washstands, pie safes, glassware, and china had all lost their luster.

Finding an old typewriter all in one piece was a real coup. Finding two and having a brother-in-law willing to hand deliver them back to Nashville—because I'd flown down for the visit—well, there are no words.

Because I had let that opportunity to get a little straw hat in Minnie's museum slip through my fingers, I learned my lesson. Don't dilly-dally and let a good opportunity pass you by. So now, I have two old manuals, and each typewriter has a special place in my home. The Royal sits on my Queen Anne secretary. (Sometimes you can tell how old a woman is by her style of furniture, and my Queen Anne definitely puts me in the "I could have been a hippie, but I joined a sorority instead" category of the early '70s. This particular brand of furniture was crafted in Nashville, so I can personally name one sister, three Nashville friends, and one sorority sister in Savannah, Georgia, who all have the same piece.) The Underwood is in the back bedroom on a round, clawfoot table inherited from my husband's grandmother.

It was only last year, when I moved my latest computer into the back bedroom, next to the table where the rougher Underwood sits, that I noticed the little white price tag left dangling from the end of the return carriage. It's the same kind of price tag Minnie Pearl always used on her straw hat. It's what put her on the map. And here I was, all these years later, using a computer to write, print, edit, and communicate all over the map with people I would never have seen or heard from again, had it not been for that infamous "You've got mail!" greeting.

I keep the price tag on my Underwood as a daily reminder of that special someone I met many years ago. It confirms what it is I do and why I should always have fun doing it. It keeps my ego in check, and on really bad days encourages me to proclaim, "I'm just so proud to be here!"

RICK WARWICK

The Reluctant Writer

My good friend, the late Miss Mary Trim Anderson, actually forced me to begin writing. As a bicentennial project, the Williamson County Historical Society asked members to write articles on past citizens for *The Review-Appeal* each week throughout 1976. Miss Anderson recognized a need to have articles on African-Americans, as well as the traditional white founding fathers and mothers. Knowing that I was collecting information on Williamson County's premier chairmaker, who happened to be of mixed-race, she nailed me down one afternoon in the Hillsboro School library.

Always mindful of my limitations as a writer, mainly manifested in the red-penciled themes received from my teachers, I tried to beg off. Of course, anyone knowing Miss Anderson realized that she did not suffer fools or foot-draggers lightly. Within minutes, I was assigned to write an article for the Thursday edition, with an understanding that the article would also appear in the 1977 edition of the Society's annual journal.

This assignment brought back memories of my freshman attempts at writing a term paper for Dr. William Beasley at Middle Tennessee State University in 1966. I had flashbacks of sweating BBs trying to fill up a blue book with a simple theme within the hour period. As you can imagine, I never mastered the use of the *Harbrace Handbook*. I even recalled the musty smells of the basement of the old English-department building in the center of campus, which fortunately was demolished before I left college and replaced with a more modern highrise.

Handicapped as a "hunt-and-pecker," I nonetheless began writing on the old Remington typewriter in my office. I attempted to organize the facts concerning my subject, Dick Poynor. I had my two introductory sentences: "Williamson County has been bequeathed much in the way of history, charm, and tradition. One contribution the community of Leiper's Fork can claim to this heritage is an elegant piece of furniture known as the Dick Poynor chair." All that remained was to finish filling up the rest of the page with facts concerning my subject. I had to relate the fact that Dick was born in Halifax County, Virginia, in 1802, and that he came to Williamson County in 1816 with his master, Robert Poynor. Dick had six children by Lucinda, and after her death, purchased his second wife, Millie. He learned to make chairs from his master, and after Robert's death in 1848, Dick established a chair factory on Pinewood Road, west of Leiper's Fork.

On it went until the closing paragraph, which after reading now, is not bad for a reluctant writer's first attempt:

"The construction of Poynor's works of art was simple. His mule-powered turning lathe, handsaw, brace and bit, and wood from the sugar maple and hickory were all that were needed. Newly cut maple was used for posts, and cured hickory used for the rungs. Using only two wooden pegs and the knowledge that wood shrinks as it dries out, Poynor produced a durable masterpiece. The chair's simple design and graceful arched back of golden maple with woven hickory bottom help explain why the Dick Poynor chair has become a treasured possession for all who own one."

Thirty-two years later, I find writing not as challenging, but the old haunts of comma placement, capitalization, and verb tense remain stumbling blocks. There will always be a need for my wife to proofread my writing. The old adage that practice makes perfect may not be totally true, but the confidence to try has improved.

There is something magical about transferring one's thoughts to a page with clarity, hoping the reader gets the point. Even this once-reluctant writer is willing to keep on trying.

ALANA WHITE

Find the Good

"*Mistah* Haley."

Surprise and admiration trembled in the elderly porter's voice as Alex Haley stepped from my car in front of the Nashville airport. While Dr. Haley's secretary, a tall, quiet gentleman, removed luggage from the trunk, the author of *Roots* shook the porter's hand and spoke softly with him for a moment. Then Dr. Haley turned away from the curb, starting for the terminal doors.

Sorely disappointed, I stood watching by my automobile. He had completely forgotten me. I had chatted about fiction writing from the time he climbed into my car for the short drive to the airport until a few moments ago, when we had reached our destination.

The year was 1981. Alex Haley had flown to Nashville to be the keynote speaker at a writers' conference I had helped organize. I volunteered to drive him to the airport afterward—that was how the man who had won a special Pulitzer for his fictionalized account of his African-American heritage had come to be riding in my passenger seat. Neither he nor his stoic secretary had any recourse but to at least pretend to listen while I described the novel I had struggled for so long to write. Haley had, after all, asked me what the story was about.

"A young girl growing up in the Smoky Mountains in the 1940s," I replied, describing, as we buzzed along the interstate, how *Roots* had inspired me to draw on my own emotions from the stories my grandmother told me about our people. Our ancestors had come to Kentucky and Tennessee from Virginia ages and ages ago, or so it seemed to me as a little girl listening to Mamaw on the porch swing on summer evenings out in the country.

"But it's hard," I said to this quiet, dignified man who had taught himself to write during a long career in the U.S. Coast Guard, and who had undertaken writing *The Autobiography of Malcolm X* before beginning twelve years of research for the novel that would become an American classic.

"Finding time to write and revise is difficult," I explained to him as we drove. "Keeping hold of the dream despite the rejections." My voice faltered as I spoke. "Sometimes I wonder if I should just give up."

Haley nodded, his gaze fixed on the highway ahead, his thoughts surely a million miles away, on home, on family, on his next speaking engagement. From the secretary in the backseat, there had come a prolonged sigh.

Now I stood watching as the writer I so admired approached the terminal doors. But there, suddenly, he turned, his brown eyes soft on me. "You write that book," he said. "You have it in your heart." With that, he was gone.

Often in the days that followed, as I struggled with my manuscript, I remembered Alex Haley's words to me. How could I *not* keep writing my book? In time, I did finish *Come Next Spring*, and a major house in New York published it.

Alex Haley died in 1992. Two years earlier, I had written, thanking him for his generous contribution to a literary fellowship awarded for fiction writers in Tennessee. In my letter I reminded Dr. Haley of our brief meeting almost a decade earlier and told him how very much his words had meant to me. A few days later, he replied with a handwritten note of thanks. The bottom of his letterhead bore a quote: "Find the good—and praise it."

Over time, what I have learned about the writing life and about life in general is that it is almost never easy. Each of us, at some point, faces hardships and rejection. What we must always remember is to have faith in ourselves. As Alex Haley said, we must pursue the things we hold dear in our hearts. We must find the good and praise it.

And praise people like him, too.

DORRIS CALLICOTT
DOUGLASS

One Little Pale-Face Indian Girl

"One little, two little, three little Indians"—and you know the rest, all the way up to "ten little Indian boys!" "Rich man, poor man, beggar man, thief; doctor, lawyer, Indian chief . . ." Ah, my dream was to be an Indian chief, though my daddy was a lawyer. It was the mid 1940s, and I would spend hours playing Indian in a clump of locust trees just across the driveway, but in plain view from the kitchen window. I was a "big girl" and was permitted to go outside of the yard, but only to that one spot. My brother, on the other hand, who was five years older, had full rein of our entire thirty-acre farm. He could go to the creek, and to the spring, and even to the backwoods. When I would complain in frustration over not being allowed to do the things he did, Mother had two set answers. Either she would sternly say, "You can't because you are a girl," which meant I never could, or she would smile sweetly and say, "Your day is coming."

Occasionally my brother played Indian with me, but when he did, I was informed I was a squaw, and that was that—unless I wanted to be a pale-face, and that was worse! He was the chief and had a beautiful authentic Indian war bonnet to prove it.

It was sweet that he (a future landscape architect) once brought me wild violets from the backwoods and planted them under my locust trees—but I really would have preferred eagle feathers. My brother was not the only one that insisted on my being a squaw. My grandfather always called me Minnehaha, even if I was painted up like an Indian warrior. Why couldn't I be Hiawatha?

One day, as a squaw, I filled my old iron black kettle with water. I then built an Indian fireplace of a circle of rocks and put the kettle in the center (but there was no real fire, mind you). My Indian-chief brother got on his horse, Sunshine, rode off, and then came galloping back. He stopped, aimed his rifle, and shot a hole right in my kettle! I stood there, watching the water trickle out of the ruined kettle, but I didn't cry—for, deep down, I was a chief, too!

On the outside of the backyard fence there were lots of poke plants with berries that were perfect for Indian war paint. I would squash the berries on my face and smear the purple juice with my finger in long streaks down my cheeks. I was very careful to wash my hands afterward, for I had been told time and time again that poke plants were poisonous, except for the leaves that were used to make poke salad. I later learned that my mother had been mistaken. It is the roots that are poisonous and not the berries at all.

I found an empty tow sack down in the basement, where we parked the cars, one behind the other. My grandfather's car was a dark-blue 1941 Plymouth, one of the last cars off the assembly line before the war. (Today when I say "the war," my grown kids grin at me and say, "Which war?") I sat down on the dirt basement floor, near our coal-burning furnace, with that tow sack. I cut the sack apart and pulled out several strings on each end to give it a fringe. I took some poke berries and painted a zigzag border on either end, squashing one berry after another. I remember how nice and cool it was there that hot summer day, just like air conditioning today.

ONE LITTLE PALE-FACE INDIAN GIRL

I had no Indian headdress, so I made my own. And when it tore up, I made another, and another. I would cut a strip from what I called colored drawing paper, but what they called construction paper at school. I usually used brown. I would Scotch-tape the ends together, making a band to fit snuggly around my head, and would then go find me a white chicken feather to put in the back. The chickens gathered under the plum trees in the backyard, and there were plenty of feathers on the ground. I went barefoot all summer long and learned to avoid the chicken doo, but occasionally I had it ooze between my toes. (I learned from my big brother how to wipe my feet clean in the grass, which worked especially well if it was early morning and the grass was still wet.) My paper headdress never would work well with more than one feather, so I was stuck with being a brave and not a chief.

There was one day I didn't get to play Indian, when Mr. Drumright, who lived behind us on Old Hickory Boulevard, paid us a visit. He had once come to visit us on his horse, riding up through the backwoods, but this day he drove up in his car. A mad dog was in the neighborhood, he told my parents, and we children would have to stay inside. My parents explained to me that the dog wasn't mad, but had hydrophobia, the common term for rabies back then, and it would be foaming at the mouth. A child at school told me later that if you got bit, you had to take awful shots with a huge needle in the stomach every day for two weeks. An Indian chief would have faced those shots bravely, I thought.

I'll never forget the day the Sears and Roebuck catalog came in the mail! My mother and I sat on the front porch, side by side on the glider, slowly turning each page of the children's section. There, on one of the pages, was an Indian suit, war bonnet and all. Of course, there was also a squaw outfit. I begged and begged for the Indian suit, and she argued and argued for the squaw outfit.

"Why do you want the Indian suit and not the Indian dress? Look, the girl's jacket has fringe on the sleeves just like the boy's, and there is fringe all around the skirt," she said. "Is it the war bonnet? I can order you a war bonnet by itself to wear with the dress."

"No, I want the suit with the Indian pants," I insisted.

My sweet mother gave in and ordered the Indian suit. I thought it would never come. When it finally did, it was a real hot day, but I wore it anyway and got soaked with sweat in the long sleeves and pants. Mother washed it and folded it up and put it in the drawer. I don't think I ever wore it again before I grew out of it. But I romped and whooped with the Indian war bonnet for a couple of years.

The farm where the little pale-face Indian spent many happy days in the 1940s is now covered with cluster homes of the Brentwood subdivision called Copperfield. My childhood home, built by my father in 1938, is still there, though its floor plan has changed, and a new generation of children romp and whoop in its living room.

I have a granddaughter now who likes to play with Hot Wheels cars. My son-in-law disapproves, for she is his little princess, and cars are boy toys. But her "Nanna" has cars for her to play with. And as I watch her line them up, I often think of her great-grandmother, long deceased, who allowed me to be an Indian chief.

SUSIE SIMS IRVIN

The River

I live in the bend of the river.
She circles round behind me
and holds me in.

My front fields lead out to the highway
but coming home is to the river.

She is my good neighbor
who just keeps riding by
sometimes laughing as she slings
whitewater down rapids
or lazily rolls over drifting logs
sometimes sliding by smoothlike
a lady whose white birches arch
over her . . . wild buttercup and phlox
press in upon her thighs.

It is summer now.
She lies flat
rocky ribs gape as she retches
over stagnant pool, warm green scum
and buzzing dragonfly.
But winter rains resuscitate and
soon she will sneak past the rock wall
sprawl across the low fields.
Shimmer like a sunning snake.
Claim *these too are yet mine*.

ABOUT THE AUTHORS

Christopher Allen, a native of Williamson County, completed an MA in English at Middle Tennessee State University where he was named Graduate Student of the Year in 1994. He won the Neal D. Frazier Writing Award for his essay "The Myth of Masculine Conscience," and a Peck Award for outstanding achievement in the study of literature at MTSU. His poems "I Dreamed We Dreamed A Dream" and "The End All," as well as the short story "Air-conditioned Souls," have appeared in university publications. An instructor and translator, Allen writes Southern literary fiction, humor/satire, and pedagogical material. He currently resides in Munich, Germany.

Nancy Evelyn Allen, MACE, is the author of the book series *The Covenant Woman*. *The Covenant Woman: Growing the Church* won second place at the 2007 Blue Ridge Mountains Christian Writers Conference, and *The Covenant Woman: Created and Chosen* won first place in 2008. She writes a bimonthly column for the *Nolensville Dispatch* and the *Eagleville Times*, and recorded 87 vignettes for WNAH Christian Talk Radio. She has also written a novel, *Daddy Alb*. Allen graduated from Southern Baptist Theological Seminary and is a member of the Tennessee Writers Alliance. She lives in Nolensville, Tennessee.

Madison Smartt Bell, a native of Williamson County, is the author of twelve novels and two collections of stories. *All Souls' Rising* was a finalist for the National Book Award and the PEN/Faulkner Award for Fiction. He is also the recipient of the Williamson County Council for the Written Word Hall of Fame award. Bell's story "June 1864" is an excerpt from his novel *Devil's Dream* which will be published in the fall of 2009. A professor of English and the director of the Kratz Center for Creative Writing at Goucher College, Bell lives in Baltimore, Maryland.

About the Authors

Angela Britnell writes romantic fiction, and her first novel *Truth and Consequence* was published in 2006. She is a member of the Romantic Novelists' Association and the Romance Writers of America. Britnell grew up in Cornwall, England, and after meeting her American husband in Denmark, traveled widely with his Navy career and now lives in Franklin, Tennessee.

Suzanne Brunson has a journalism degree from the University of Georgia. She has toiled through the years as a newspaper editor, reporter, occasional columnist, Vanderbilt fundraiser, and freelance writer. She has written one historical fiction novel, and her short stories have appeared in *Muscadine Lines: A Southern Journal*. She is a member of the Tennessee Writers Alliance and currently serves as Corresponding Secretary for the Williamson County Council for the Written Word. Brunson lives in Brentwood, Tennessee.

Chance Chambers was a top 100 winner in the Mainstream/Literary Short Story category of the Writer's Digest 73rd Annual Writing Competition for his story "Miss October." He has also been a quarter-finalist for Francis Ford Coppola's *Zoetrope: All-Story* and New Century Writer Awards for short story, a finalist for *Glimmer Train*'s Poetry Open, and a three-time nominee for the Sensored Starving Artist awards in fiction and poetry. Originally from Paris, Tennessee, Chambers has lived in Nashville since 1985.

Louise Colln has five nationally and internationally published books. Her poetry, articles, and short stories have been published in anthologies and national magazines. Colln is a board member of the Tennessee Writers Alliance and Secretary of the Williamson County Council for the Written Word. Having spent most of her life in Illinois and Missouri, she now lives in Franklin, Tennessee, where the natural beauty and sense of history encourage her interest in people and appreciation of the world we live in.

James A. Crutchfield has authored more than forty volumes of American history, including his first book, *The Harpeth River: A Biography*, and his latest, *Tribute to an Artist: The Jamestown Paintings of Sidney E. King*. He has been recognized with awards from the Tennessee Revolutionary War Bicentennial Commission, Western Writers of America, the American Association for State and Local History, the Heritage Foundation of Williamson County, and is a recipient of the Williamson County Council for the Written Word Hall of Fame award. He has penned hundreds of articles for *The Magazine Antiques*, *Early American Life*, *Wild West*, *Tennessee Historical Quarterly*, and others. Crutchfield lives in Franklin, Tennessee.

Dorris Callicott Douglass, BA, MLS, is a librarian, historian, and genealogist. Head of Special Collections Department at the Williamson County Public Library, she has been the reviewer of memoirs and autobiography for the *Library Journal*, had a bimonthly column "Two Hundred Years Ago in Williamson County" in the *Williamson Herald*, and won the award for best article in the *Williamson County Historical Society Journal* one year. Douglass is also in *Who's Who of American Women*. She lives in Franklin, Tennessee.

Susie Dunham, former columnist for the *Grassland Gazette* and *Westview* newspapers, writes creative nonfiction, which can be humorous or serious—depending on her mood at the keyboard. Her stories "Parlor Cowboys" and "Tick Attack in Tennessee" appeared in *Muscadine Lines: A Southern Anthology*. Dunham also enjoys improv and hopes someday to belong to an improv troupe, proving that it's never too late to try new things. Born and raised in upstate New York, Dunham currently lives in Franklin, Tennessee.

About the Authors

Linda McClure Dunn, born in Louisiana, channeled her love of words as a child into stories for school projects and personal diaries. Over the years she has written for local newspapers and used her writing talents in volunteer work, only recently beginning to pursue writing seriously. A self-described crone, her life experiences provide material for her poetry, introspective prose, and memoir. Her work has appeared in *Muscadine Lines: A Southern Journal*. Dunn is a member of the Tennessee Writers Alliance, National Association for Poetry Therapy, Creative Nonfiction Foundation, and Women Who Write Loudly. She resides in Franklin, Tennessee.

Nancy Fletcher-Blume served three years as president of the Tennessee Writers Alliance, nine years as president of the Williamson County Council for the Written Word, and is now serving as CWW Chairman of the Board. She is the recipient of the 2009 Council for the Written Word Jane Langston Service Award. She won the Kay Tricki Award which led to the publication of a children's book *The Cast Iron Dogs*, and was published in *Our Voices: Williamson County Literary Review* 1995, 1997, and 1998. She condensed and adapted two children's classics for Dalmatian Press: Robert Louis Stevenson's *Kidnapped* and *Treasure Island*. She is co-author of a Civil War poetry book, *Echoes of Two Voices*. Her poem "In Two Voices" was read at the Romanian Writers Festival in 2005. Fletcher-Blume, a native of South Carolina, lives in Franklin, Tennessee.

Tom T. Hall, known to countless country music fans as "The Storyteller," was born in Olive Hill, Kentucky, in a log house built by his grandfather. Among his earlier books are a memoir-history, *The Storyteller's Nashville*, and a novel, *The Laughing Man of Woodmont Coves*. Hall is a recipient of the Williamson County Council for the Written Word Hall of Fame award. He lives with his wife, Dixie, on a farm in Franklin, Tennessee, where he is at work on a second novel and songs for a new album.

Robert Hicks, author of *New York Times* best seller *The Widow of the South*, was born and raised in South Florida. He moved to Williamson County, Tennessee, in 1974, and lives near the Bingham community at *Labor in Vain*, his late-eighteenth-century log cabin. He was co-editor of the critically acclaimed catalog *Art of Tennessee*. *The Tennessean* named him Tennessean of the Year in 2005. He also co-edited *A Guitar and a Pen: Stories by Country Music's Greatest Songwriters*. Hicks received the Williamson County Council for the Written Word Hall of Fame award in 2007. His second novel, *A Separate Country*, will be released in September 2009.

Susie Sims Irvin was born in Nashville, Tennessee, and moved to Franklin after her marriage to Shearer Irvin. Many of her Franklin years were spent on a farm that is now part of the Fieldstone Farms subdivision. A graduate of Vanderbilt University, she studied with Fugitive poet Donald Davidson. In 2003, Irvin was inducted into the Williamson County Council for the Written Word Hall of Fame. She is the author of *Too Tall Alice*, *Clouds for the Table*, *Falls Even Now the Seed*, and *SHHH... It's Time for the Devotional*.

Madison Percy Jones was born in Nashville, Tennessee, and attended Vanderbilt University and the University of Florida. He taught English at Miami University, University of Tennessee, and Auburn University, where he is professor emeritus. He has been awarded a *Sewanee Review* fellowship, an Alabama Library Association Book Award, a Rockefeller fellowship, a Guggenheim fellowship, the Andrew Lytle Prize for short fiction, and was inducted into the Williamson County Council for the Written Word Hall of Fame. Jones is the author of ten novels, including *The Innocent*, *Forest of the Night*, *Season of the Strangler*, *A Cry of Absence*, *A Buried Land*, *Nashville 1864: The Dying of the Light*, and *An Exile*, which was adapted for the 1970 film *I Walk the Line*. Jones lives in Auburn, Alabama.

About the Authors

S.R. Lee writes both prose and poetry. She has spent her lifetime in Middle Tennessee and lives on the family farm in Williamson County. She is the author of *Granny Lindy; Beechville: Then, Now and In Between*; and *Spirit of Monterey*. She is contributing editor of *The Poets of St. Paul's*, an anthology of St. Paul's Episcopal Church, Franklin, Tennessee. She has also been honored by the Council for the Written Word with the Jane Langston Service Award. Lee draws her themes both from the immediacy of home and from flights of the imagination.

Ginger Manley is an award-winning writer in several genres, including academic medicine, creative nonfiction, historical tracts, and fiction. Her first novel, *Proud Flesh*—a poignant tale of sex, God, and the redemptive power of buck dancing—is awaiting a publisher. She has edited *Gotcha Covered*, an anthology of The Nurses' Apron Partnership, and is currently writing her first nonfiction book. She writes "Assisted Loving," a monthly sexual advice column for those not quite ready for assisted living, which appears in *Mature Lifestyles*. Her experiences as a nurse and certified sex therapist, a parent and grandparent, a golfer, and a gardener provide ample sources for her creative musings. Manley is a seventh-generation Tennessean and an associate professor of psychiatry at Vanderbilt Medical Center. She lives in Franklin, Tennessee.

Olive Mayger, a native of the Upper Peninsula of Michigan, has lived in Williamson County, Tennessee, for over a quarter of a century. After a career in private and public education that included both classroom teaching and administration, she currently concentrates on teaching theatre for children, facilitating local theatre productions, and writing. She is a graduate of The Writer's Loft of Middle Tennessee State University and holds a BA and MA in education. Mayger lives in Franklin, Tennessee.

Laurie Michaud-Kay began a career in writing because she was curious. Writing provided an excuse for digging deeper into subjects, both human and academic. After obtaining degrees in both English and history from Adrian College, she turned this personality quirk into a seventeen-year career in public relations and internal communications, earning individual awards for writing and design, and a team Silver Anvil Award from the Public Relations Society of America. Now retired, Michaud-Kay lives in Franklin, Tennessee, where she has returned to crafting creative nonfiction, essays, and short stories drawn from the meandering of her curiosity.

Carroll Chambers Moth, a transplant from New York, is a newly retired teacher of Visual Arts. She is a member of the Tennessee Writers Alliance, the Puppet Guild of Long Island, Puppeteers of America, and UNIMA-USA. She is currently writing haiku poetry as well as a variety of somewhat twisted short stories. Moth lives in Fairview, Tennessee.

Bill Peach is the author of four books: *To Think As a Pawn*; *The South Side of Boston*; *Random Thoughts Left & Right*; and, most recently, *Politics, Preaching & Philosophy* with Westview Publishing, which includes short essays from his columns for the *Williamson Herald*. He is a member of the Williamson County School Board and is Chairman Emeritus for the Williamson County Council for the Written Word. He was inducted into CWW's Hall of Fame in 2001. Peach, a semi-retired men's clothier, is a native of Boston, Tennessee. He lives in Franklin, Tennessee.

About the Authors

Currie Alexander Powers was born in Toronto, Canada. She is the author of the novel *Soul of a Man*, and her writing has appeared in *Muscadine Lines: A Southern Anthology* and *Tin House*. As a musician, she has played and recorded with Bruce Cockburn, Rick Danko, and Stephen Fearing, and her songs have been recorded by Sara Craig and Blackie & The Rodeo Kings, among others. She is working on her second novel, *Running from the Button Moulder*, and continues to write songs. Powers lives in Nashville, Tennessee.

Kathy Hardy Rhodes is a board member of the Tennessee Writers Alliance and President of the Williamson County Council for the Written Word. She is author of *Pink Butterbeans: Stories from the heart of a Southern woman*; publisher and editor of the online magazine *Muscadine Lines: A Southern Journal*, currently in its fifth year; and editor of the book *Muscadine Lines: A Southern Anthology*. Rhodes is also a regular facilitator for Writers' Roundtable at Barnes & Noble, Cool Springs. Her writing has appeared in *Our Voices: Williamson County Literary Review*, 1995, 1997, and 1998, *The Oxford So and So*, and The Writer's Loft's *The Trunk*. Her essay "The Wedding Hankie" was included in Simon & Schuster's *Chocolate for a Woman's Soul II*. Her essay "An Open Letter" is forthcoming in *The Best Creative Nonfiction Volume 3*, published by W.W. Norton, in the summer of 2009. Born and raised in the Mississippi Delta, Rhodes lives in Franklin, Tennessee.

James E. Robinson is an award-winning songwriter, author, therapist, and speaker. His songs have been recorded by country, pop, and Christian artists. Midwest Book Review called his first book, *Prodigal Song: A Memoir* (2003), ". . . a moving and life-affirming portrayal, spiritually rewarding and reader inspiring." His first novel, *The Flower of Grass*, was released by Monarch/Kregel in 2008. Born in Camden, Tennessee, Robinson now lives in Franklin, Tennessee.

David B. Stewart, a native of Northwest Arkansas, spent most of his life in Texas and Oklahoma. His mother's family had set roots in Williamson and Maury Counties at least two generations before he arrived in the area. He credits that Brewer family line for his talents that include poetry, prose, and art. Once a budding broadcast journalist, he chose engineering as a profession. Writing for a hobby and pleasure saves him from the monotony of technology and gives his children and grandchild something to puzzle at. Stewart lives in Franklin, Tennessee.

Jim Taulman has served as a pastor, editor, and personal historian. In each position he has combined his love for writing and speaking. He was educated at Oklahoma Baptist University (BA), Southern Baptist Theological Seminary (MDiv and ThM), with a year's clinical pastoral education at Bethesda Hospital, Cincinnati, Ohio, and journalistic studies at Ohio State University. He has written *Encouragers: The Sunday School Worker's Counseling Ministry*; *Help! I Need an Idea*; *Never Tell Anybody Anything You Can Get Them to Discover for Themselves*; and *My Word: Taultales by a Taulman*. He has assisted others in writing personal memoirs and has also written more than 1,000 articles and anthems. Taulman lives in Franklin, Tennessee.

Paula Wall is the national-bestselling author of four books. Her first novel, *The Rock Orchard*, was a Book Sense pick and was named as a Barnes & Noble Discover Great New Writers title. Her latest novel, *The Wilde Women*, is a Book Club pick. She is a recipient of the Williamson County Council for the Written Word Hall of Fame award. Wall lives in Fernvale, Tennessee.

About the Authors

Rick Warwick spent many years as a classroom teacher and school librarian. He now applies his energy to collecting the history of Williamson County. He has been publication chairman of the Williamson County Historical Society since 1990, and has published the annual journal, as well as projects of his own choosing. This body of work includes *Williamson County in Black and White*; *Historical Markers of Williamson County, Tennessee: A Pictorial Guide*; and *A Century of Chairmakers in Williamson County*. Warwick graduated from Middle Tennessee State University (BS, MAT) and has served on the Tennessee Historical Commission since 2005. He is also the recipient of the Williamson County Council for the Written Word Hall of Fame award. Warwick lives in Franklin, Tennessee.

Mary Ann Weakley was born and raised in Illinois, attended Marycrest College, Davenport, Iowa, and received her master's degree from the University of Illinois. After years of teaching in Illinois, she moved to Williamson County, Tennessee, where she began an interior design business. She continues interior design while beginning a third career as a writer. Weakley's writing can be found online and in a monthly column for *The Informer: Community News* of Spring Hill. Her first book, a memoir in progress, draws on her experiences within an Illinois convent. She lives in Spring Hill, Tennessee.

Alana White is the author of *Come Next Spring*, a novel set in 1940s Appalachia, and a biography, *Sacagawea: Westward with Lewis and Clark*. She is also the author of Macavity-nominated historical mystery short stories and writes nonfiction and book reviews for *Renaissance Magazine* and for the Historical Novel Society. White lives in Nashville, Tennessee.

Printed in the United States
220407BV00002B/2/P